Δ The Triangle Papers: 33

Restoring Growth in the Debt-Laden Third World

A Task Force Report to
The Trilateral Commission

Authors: MARTIN FELDSTEIN
President, National Bureau of
Economic Research, Inc.;
George F. Baker Professor of Economics,
Harvard University;
Former Chairman,
U.S. Council of Economic Advisers

HERVÉ DE CARMOY
Director and Chief Executive International,
Midland Bank

KOEI NARUSAWA
Economic Advisor to the President,
Bank of Tokyo

PAUL R. KRUGMAN
Professor of Economics,
Massachusetts Institute of Technology

© Copyright, 1987. The Trilateral Commission

Library of Congress Cataloging-in-Publication Data

Restoring growth in the debt-laden Third World

(Triangle papers ; 33)
"April 1987."
Bibliography: p.
1. Debts, External—Developing countries. 2. Developing countries—Economic policy. I. Feldstein, Martin S. II. Trilateral Commission. III. Series.
HJ8899.R47   1987   336.3'435'091724   87-23778
ISBN 0930503-02-3

Manufactured in the United States of America

THE TRILATERAL COMMISSION

| 345 East 46th Street
New York, N.Y. 10017 | c/o Japan Center for
International Exchange
4-9-17 Minami-Azabu
Minato-ku
Tokyo, Japan | 35, avenue de Friedland
75008 Paris, France |

The Authors

MARTIN FELDSTEIN is the George F. Baker Professor of Economics at Harvard University and President of the National Bureau of Economic Research. From 1982 through 1984, he was Chairman of the Council of Economic Advisers and President Reagan's Chief Economic Adviser. After graduating from Harvard College in 1961, Dr. Feldstein studied at Oxford University where he became a member of the faculty and a fellow of Nuffield College and received his doctor of philosophy degree in 1967. He joined the Harvard faculty that year and became Professor of Economics in 1969. Dr. Feldstein is the author of more than 200 scientific articles on a wide range of economic subjects. He is a regular contributor to the *Wall Street Journal*. He and his wife, who is also an economist, write a monthly column for the *Washington Post* and the *Los Angeles Times* syndicate.

HERVÉ DE CARMOY is Director and Chief Executive International of Midland Bank. He joined the bank in 1978, first as Chairman of the Executive Board of Midland Bank, France. He added the title of General Manager, London in 1979; and in 1980 took on a leading role in the revival of a Midland acquisition in Germany, the banking house of Trinkus and Burkhardt. He became Chief Executive of the International Division of Midland Bank in 1984, and added the task of Director in 1986. Educated at the Sorbonne (including at the Institute of Political Science) and Cornell University (M.B.A., 1960), Mr. Carmoy began his career with Chase Manhattan Bank. He was Vice President and General Manager of Chase Manhattan Bank France in 1971-73, and Regional President, Chase Manhattan Bank Western Europe, in 1973-78. Mr. Carmoy is a Fulbright and Telluride Scholar.

KOEI NARUSAWA is Economic Advisor to the President of the Bank of Tokyo, a position he has held since 1980. A graduate of Tokyo Imperial University's Department of Jurisprudence, Mr. Narusawa joined the Bank of Tokyo in 1948. He subsequently served as General Manager of the Hamburg office (1969-70) and then in the London office (1971-72). In 1972, he returned to Tokyo to become General Manager of the Economic Research Division, rising in 1973 to Director and in 1976 to Managing Director. His publications include recent articles entitled *The Prospects of International Finance in 1987* and *The Prospects of the Japanese Economy in 1987* (both in Japanese). He is a member, and chairman since 1985, of the International Conference of Commercial Bank Economists; and was a member of the International Club of Bank Economists from 1980 to 1985.

PAUL R. KRUGMAN is Professor of Economics at the Massachusetts Institute of Technology. Educated at Yale University and MIT (Ph.D., 1977), Dr. Krugman first taught at Yale and then joined the MIT faculty in 1980. In 1982-83 he was an International Policy Economist on the staff of the President's Council of Economic Advisers. He has been a Research Associate at the National Bureau of Economic Research since 1978. He has been Rapporteur of the Panel on Advanced Technology Competition and the Industrialized Allies, of the National Academy of Sciences, since 1981. Prof. Krugman's extensive list of publications includes contributions to many aspects of international economics. His books include *Market Structure and Foreign Trade* (with E. Helpman, 1985). His articles include "International Debt Strategies in an Uncertain World" (in J. Cuddington and R. Smith, eds., *The World Debt Problem*, World Bank, 1985).

The Trilateral Process

The report which follows is the joint responsibility of its four authors. Martin Feldstein had principal responsibility, while Hervé de Carmoy and Paul Krugman shouldered major drafting tasks. Although only the authors are responsible for the analysis and conclusions, they have been aided in their work by many others. The persons consulted spoke for themselves as individuals and not as representatives of any institutions with which they are associated. Those consulted or otherwise assisting in the development of the report included the following:

Naohiro Amaya, *Special Advisor to the Minister of International Trade and Industry; President, Japan Economic Foundation*

Giovanni Auletta Armenise, *Chairman, Banca Nazionale dell'Agricoltura, Rome*

Piero Bassetti, *Chairman, IPALMO, Rome*

Georges Berthoin, *European Chairman, Trilateral Commission; International Honorary Chairman, European Movement*

Rodric Braithwaite, *Foreign & Commonwealth Office, London*

Richard Brantner, *Kreditanstalt für Wiederaufbau, Frankfurt*

Jean-Claude Casanova, *Professor of Economics, Institute of Political Studies; Editor,* Commentaire, *Paris*

Gail C.A. Cook, *Executive Vice President, Bennecon Ltd., Toronto*

Philippe Coste, *Director of the Policy Planning Staff, Ministry of Foreign Affairs, Paris*

Alain Cotta, *Professor of Economics and Management, University of Paris*

David M. Culver, *Chairman and Chief Executive Officer, Alcan Aluminum Limited, Montreal*

Jean Deflassieux, *Honorary Chairman, Crédit Lyonnais, Paris*

Paul Delouvrier, *Parc de la Villette; former Chairman, French Electricity Board*

Peter C. Dobell, *Director, Parliamentary Centre for Foreign Affairs and Foreign Trade, Ottawa*

Thomas O. Enders, *Managing Director, Salomon Brothers; former U.S.Ambassador to Spain and Assistant Secretary of State for Inter-American Affairs*

Pierre Esteva, *Honorary Chairman, Union des Assurances de Paris*

Paul Fabra, *Senior Columnist,* Le Monde *, Paris*

Gianandrea Falchi, *Head of Research Department, National Bank of Italy, Rome*

A. Fernandez-Villaverde, *Director, Banco Hispano Americano, Madrid*

René Foch, *Honorary Director General, Commission of the European Communities, Paris*

Antonio Garrigues Walker, *President, Democratic Reform Party, Madrid*

Alan Greenspan, *President, Townsend-Greenspan & Company, Incorporated; former Chairman, U.S. Council of Economic Advisers*

Jacques Groothaert, *Chairman, Société Générale de Banque, Brussels; Honorary Ambassador of Belgium*

Sumio Hara, *Executive Advisor, Bank of Tokyo, Ltd.*

Charles B. Heck, *North American Director, Trilateral Commission*

Stephane Hessel, *Ambassadeur de France, Paris*

Dieter Hoffmann, *Former Chairman, Neue Heimat, Hamburg*

Richard C. Holbrooke, *Managing Director, Shearson Lehman Brothers Inc.; former Assistant Secretary of State for East Asian and Pacific Affairs*

Takashi Hosomi, *Chairman, Overseas Economic Cooperation Fund*

Ludwig Huber, *Chairman, Bayerische Landesbank und Girozentrale, Munich*

Philippe Huet, *Inspecteur General des Finances, Paris*

Karl Kaiser, *Director, Research Institute of the German Society for Foreign Affairs, Bonn; Professor, University of Cologne*

Yusuke Kashiwagi, *Chairman, Bank of Tokyo, Ltd.*

Walter Leisler Kiep, *General Managing Partner, Goldman & Holler, Frankfurt; Treasurer, Christian Democratic Party*

Jeane Kirkpatrick, *American Enterprise Institute for Public Policy Research; former U.S. Ambassador to the United Nations*

Norbert Kloten, *Member of the Central Bank Council of the German Bundesbank, Stuttgart*

Charles Kovacs, *Vice President, Chase Manhattan Bank, N.A.*

Juan Pablo Laiglesia, *Director General, Latin America Department, Ministry of Foreign Affairs, Madrid*

Roger Lavelle, *United Kingdom Treasury, London*

Jim Leach, *Member of U.S. House of Representatives*

James T. Lynn, *Chairman, Aetna Life and Casualty Co.*

Patra Mateos, *Deputy Director General, Banco Exterior de España, Madrid*

Hanns Maull, *Assistant Professor of Political Science, University of Munich*

Bruce K. MacLaury, *President, Brookings Institution*

Cesare Merlini, *Chairman, Institute for International Affairs, Rome*

Thierry de Montbrial, *Director, French Institute for International Relations, Paris*

Sir Jeremy Morse, *Chairman, Lloyds Bank*

Gilbert Mourre, *Deputy Director General, Caisse Centrale de Cooperation Economique, Paris*

Martin Murtfeldt, *Deutsche Bank, Frankfurt*

Toshio Nakamura, *Chairman, Mitsubishi Bank, Ltd.*

Sumio Okahashi, *Senior Advisor, Sumitomo Corporation*

Yoshio Okawara, *Executive Advisor, Keidanren (Federation of Economic Organizations in Japan); former Ambassador to the United States*

Saburo Okita, *Chairman, Institute for Domestic and International Policy Studies (IDIPS); former Minister for Foreign Affairs*

Ariyoshi Okumura, *Director and Chief Financial Economist, Industrial Bank of Japan, Ltd.*

Egidio Ortona, *European Deputy Chairman, Trilateral Commission*

Sir Michael Palliser, *Chairman, Samuel Montagu & Co., London*

Karl-Otto Pöhl, *President, Deutsche Bundesbank, Frankfurt*

Konrad Porzner, *Member of the German Bundestag (Manager, Social Democratic Party Parliamentary Fraction)*

Lionel Price, *Bank of England, London*

Giuseppe Ratti, *Chairman, Institute for Foreign Trade, Rome*

Paul Révay, *European Director, Trilateral Commission*

Elliot R. Richardson, *Partner, Milbank, Tweed, Hadley & McCloy*

William Rhodes, *Group Executive and Chairman of the Restructuring Committee, Citibank*

Kurt Richolt, *Commerzbank, Frankfurt*

Charles W. Robinson, *Chairman, Energy Transition Corporation; former U.S. Deputy Secretary of State*

David Rockefeller, *North American Chairman, The Trilateral Commission*

Felix G. Rohatyn, *Partner, Lazard Frères and Company*

François de Rose, *Ambassadeur de France, Paris*

Jeffrey Sachs, *Professor of Economics, Harvard University*

Kiichi Saeki, *Special Advisor, Nomura Research Institute*

A. Sanchez Pedreno, *Director General, National Bank of Spain*

Lord Sandon, *Deputy Chairman, National Westminster Bank, London*

Mario Schimberni, *Chairman, Montedison, Milan*

Pedro Schwartz, *Director, Iberagentes Brokers; Professor of Economics, Madrid University*

William W. Scranton, *Former Governor of Pennsylvania; former U.S. Ambassador to the United Nations*

Jose Antonio Segurado, *Member of Spanish Parliament; President of the Liberal Party*

Lord Shackleton, *Rio Tinto Zinc Corporation, London*

Peter Shore, *Member of British Parliament (Shadow Chancellor of the Exchequer)*

Bernard Snoy, *Councillor of the Commission of the European Communities on International Debt Issues, Brussels*

Anthony Solomon, *Chairman of the Board, S.G. Warburg (USA) Incorporated; former President of the Federal Reserve Bank of New York*

Robert S. Strauss, *Partner, Akin, Gump, Strauss, Hauer & Feld; former U.S. Special Trade Representative*

Niels Thygesen, *Professor of Economics, Copenhagen University*

Sir Crispin Tickell, *Overseas Development Administration, London*

Toshihiro Tomabechi, *Vice Chairman, Mitsubishi Motors Corporation*

Seiki Tozaki, *Chairman, C. Itoh & Co., Ltd.*

Ramon Trias Fargas, *Member of the Spanish Senate; Deputy Mayor of Barcelona*

Antonio Vasco de Mello, *Member of the Portuguese Parliament*

Sir Fred Warner, *Chairman, Trade and Investment Committee, Confederation of British Industry, London*

Kiichi Watanabe, *President, Japan Center for International Finance*

Takeshi Watanabe, *President, Japan Credit-Rating Agency; former President, Asian Development Bank*

Edmund Wellenstein, *Former Director General, Commission of the European Communities, The Hague*

Walter B. Wriston, *Former Chairman, Citicorp*

Tadashi Yamamoto, *Japanese Director, Trilateral Commission*

Isamu Yamashita, *Japanese Chairman, Trilateral Commission; Senior Advisor, Mitsui Engineering and Shipbuilding Co., Ltd.*

Sir Philip de Zulueta, *Chairman, Tanks Consolidated Investments, London*

SCHEDULE OF TASK FORCE ACTIVITIES:

May 20, 1986 — Feldstein, de Carmoy and Narusawa meet in Madrid, in wings of Trilateral Commission plenary meeting, to discuss broad thrust of report.

June and July — De Carmoy and Narusawa submit papers to Feldstein.

July 15 — Narusawa meet with Takashi Hosomi and Kiichi Watanabe in Tokyo.

July 25 — De Carmoy meets with Italian members and experts Rome.

September 11 — De Carmoy meets with French members and experts in Paris.

September 15 — De Carmoy meets with British members and experts in London.

September — Feldstein prepares outline of report; de Carmoy submits revision of his paper.

September 30 — Feldstein and de Carmoy meet in Washington.

October 13 — De Carmoy meets with Spanish members and experts in Madrid.

October 14 — Feldstein and Narusawa meet in Cambridge, Massachusetts.

October 18 — De Carmoy discusses report with European members at European regional meeting in The Hague.

November 12 — Narusawa and de Carmoy meet in London.

November 17 — De Carmoy discusses report with German members and experts in Frankfurt.

December 4 — Feldstein and Krugman meet with North American members and experts in New York.

December 19 — Narusawa meets with Japanese members and experts in Tokyo.

December — De Carmoy prepares second revision of his submission, incorporating major elements of overall discussion.

January 1987 — Krugman completes rough overall draft.

January 15 — Feldstein and de Carmoy meet in Paris.

January 22 — Feldstein, Narusawa and Yusuke Kashiwagi meet in Tokyo.

late January — De Carmoy prepares overall draft incorporating major sections of his earlier submission and of Krugman draft.

February — Narusawa and de Carmoy meet in Paris.

mid-February — Feldstein and Krugman complete San Francisco meeting draft, which is circulated to Trilateral Commission members.

March 21 — Draft report discussed in Trilateral Commission plenary meeting in San Francisco.
late April — Feldstein completes post-meeting draft.
June — Final revisions completed.

Table of Contents

Tables and Figures

INTRODUCTION

It has been five years since the foreign debt of developing countries emerged as a major policy concern. So far events have not fulfilled the expectations of either the optimists or the pessimists. We have not, as many feared in 1982, seen a collapse of the international financial system. On the other hand, many had expected that over time the debt issue would fade away, and that both normal access to capital markets and healthy economic growth in debtor nations would resume; and that has not happened either. The debt of developing countries has remained as a constant source of worry both to bankers and governments.

In our view, the core of this problem is the need to restore adequate growth rates in debtor nations. As long as debtor growth remains slow and living standards in the developing world continue to stagnate or decline, the overhang of debt will continue to present important risks to the stability of the international economy. The inadequate performance of debtor economies will lead to continuing domestic pressures for drastic unilateral action to reduce the debt burden, with an attendant risk to world financial stability; the stagnation of developing country trade will contribute to the world trade problem, and hence to protectionist pressures; and the political and security risks arising from economic dissatisfaction may rise.

Growth in the debtor countries is at least as much dependent on those countries' own policies as on external financing. This report, however, is addressed primarily to an audience representing advanced creditor nations and thus we feel it inappropriate to devote much of it to lecturing developing countries on their policies. The issue of economic policies in the debtors cannot be completely avoided, since any financial plan must be contingent on responsible action on the part of the debtors. Similarly, debtor governments must take steps to encourage a return of flight capital and to prevent further capital flight. Nonetheless, our main focus in this report will be on the options available to the creditors, both public and private.

Chapter I offers a brief review of the attempts to manage LDC debt since the emergence of the debt crisis in 1982. These attempts have had at their core a basic approach—a combination of concerted

lending by banks with IMF-monitored adjustment by debtor nations—
that we call the "1983 strategy." The "Baker initiative" of October
1985 represents an extension of this strategy, but with an emphasis on
the need to finance debtor country growth.

Chapter II sets forth a conceptual framework for thinking about
the debt situation. The key issue is the need to balance the claims of
creditors against the cost in economic growth if debtors are required
to transfer too large a fraction of their resources abroad. The Baker
strategy sought to find a middle ground in which significant resource
transfer was combined with rescheduling and new lending to allow a
resumption of growth at the same time that the ratio of debt to countries' ability to service it was steadily reduced. The chapter reviews
the logic underlying this strategy, as well as the difficulties that
have made its implementation less easy than expected.

Chapter III sets out the broader concerns of creditor and debtor
countries, with special emphasis on those interests of the Trilateral
countries that go beyond direct financial return.

Chapters IV, V, and VI then examine the possible dimensions of
new debt initiatives, survey a number of proposals, and set forth the
advantages and disadvantages of the variety of options available to
the creditor nations. We consider both generic classes of options and
specific proposals.

The final chapter sets out our own views about appropriate policy
in the future. While the authors of this report agree on many issues,
we also continue to have important differences; we report on these
differences in what we hope is an instructive mannner.

Although we do not agree on the precise diagnosis of the present
situation or on the policy that should be followed at the present
time, we do all agree on several important things: that each country
must be treated as a separate case in its own terms, that virtually all
of the debtor countries will need additional new credit in the years
ahead if they are to achieve satisfactory growth, and that outright
debt forgiveness is not the solution to the problem. What we disagree
about is how much credit the debtor countries will need to achieve
satisfactory growth, how willing the creditor banks will be to provide the necessary amount of credit, and what the prospects are for
substantial government funds to supplement the private lending.

Three of the authors of this report are sympathetic to the following appraisal: It is possible to restore satisfactory growth in the major Latin American debtor countries in a way that is consistent with
continued cooperation of the debtor governments and the creditor
banks. Achieving satisfactory strong growth in the major debtor coun-

tries need not require forgiveness of debt or any fundamental change in the nature of debt rescheduling. It does, however, require three things for at least the remainder of this decade and probably until the mid-1990s. First, the debts must be rolled over as they become due; there will in general be no repayments of principal during this period. Second, the interest rates charged on new loans must be very close to the banks' cost of funds and therefore often substantially below the rates implicit in the secondary market. Third, net new credit must be extended so that the debts of these countries will grow in nominal terms.

But although the debts of the major Latin American debtors must grow in nominal terms if satisfactory economic growth is to be achieved, the *relative* magnitude of that debt will decline. More specifically, even if debt grows at (say) 4 percent a year, that debt will be declining as a percentage of the debtors' ability to service that debt in the future. Debt will decline as a percentage of the debtor's gross national product and of the debtors' exports. Debt will be essentially constant in real inflation-adjusted terms.

This means that the debtors are not taking on an impossible burden. Similarly, it implies that although the banks' total debt exposure is growing, the banks' financial positions are actually improving over time because debt is declining as a percentage of the banks' assets and earnings and of the ability of the debtors to service that debt.

Our main concern is not about the technical feasibility of this favorable solution but about the willingness of the borrowers and creditors to act appropriately. For the debtors, there is the temptation to default or declare a moratorium. For the creditors, there is the temptation to write off existing loans and stop lending. At the present time, this temptation appears to be greater for some of the European and Japanese banks and the American regional banks than for the major American money center banks. Our judgment is that the incentives for continued satisfactory behavior by both creditors and debtors will dominate in the end, but the present risks are undeniable.

Hervé de Carmoy dissents from this optimistic prognosis and believes that satisfactory growth can only be achieved by a much more substantial infusion of new credit, provided primarily by public sources, with guaranteed credit increases for ten years. More specifically, the de Carmoy plan calls for additional new credit of $30 billion a year for ten years, a credit increase that is currently equivalent to a 10 percent rise in total credit. Half of this amount would be provided by governments of the creditor nations, one-fourth by the World Bank and other multilateral development banks, and one-fourth by the commercial banks. A new agency would be established—an Action Committee—to administer the funds and agree upon structural reform programs with the debtor nations.

The other authors of this report believe that such additional public financing is neither politically feasible nor economically necessary. The difficulty of achieving political acceptance of the need for additional financing is also fully recognized by de Carmoy. The other authors are concerned, moreover, that the suggestion that such funds might be provided could encourage unrealistic expectations and inappropriate behavior by both debtors and creditors.

I. THE DEBT PROBLEM, 1982-87

A. COMPARISONS AND CONTRASTS
AMONG DEBTOR COUNTRIES

The foreign debt of many developing countries grew rapidly from 1973 until the collapse of lender confidence in 1982. There are, however, major differences among debtors. Even countries that are often treated together, such as Brazil and Argentina, have followed very different policies in many ways. Short of treating every country separately, it is necessary at a minimum to distinguish three groups of developing country debtors for which we shall use a somewhat imprecise geographic shorthand in this report: Latin America, sub-Saharan Africa, and East Asia.

The Latin American Debtors
Most public discussion of the international debt problem focuses on the larger economies in Latin America with major debt-servicing problems. This reflects a real distinction between types of debtor experience, although one that does not quite match up with geography. In terms of the character of its debt problems, the Philippines is essentially "Latin," while some South American countries such as Colombia do not share in the debt problem.

Four aspects give the debt of these countries its salience. First, the debt is large: Brazil and Mexico alone owe about one-third of the debt to private creditors (largely to banks) of developing nations (Table 1), and a higher proportion, obviously, of the bank debt widely regarded as being at risk. Add Argentina, Venezuela and Chile and the proportion of private creditor debt covered by just these five countries is one-half of the total. Second, because this debt is held primarily by private banks the possibility of a failure to repay poses threats to the stability of the world financial system. Third, these bank loans are mostly floating rate loans and were often originally of a short-term character (one-year maturities or less).[1] Thus

---

[1]Of the total external debt for Latin America and the Carribbean at the end of 1981, about 29 percent was short term in character. The percentage was the same for the overlapping group of "highly indebted" countries.

TABLE 1

Distribution of Developing Country Debt, end of 1985
(US$ billions)

	Total External Debt[1]	Private Creditors[2]
All Developing Countries[3]	892.4 (100%)	462.8 (100%)
"Highly Indebted" Latin American Countries		
Brazil	106.7 (12%)	77.1 (17%)
Mexico	97.4 (11%)	80.6 (17%)
Argentina	48.4 (5.4%)	36.0 (7.8%)
Venezuela	32.1 (3.6%)	21.7 (4.7%)
Chile	20.2 (2.3%)	15.3 (3.3%)
Peru	13.7	7.1
Columbia	14.0	5.8
Ecuador	9.2	5.2
Uruguay	3.9	2.3
Costa Rica	4.2	2.2
Bolivia	4.0	1.2
Jamaica	3.8	.5
Other "Highly Indebted" Countries		
Philippines	26.2 (2.9%)	9.7 (2.1%)
Nigeria	18.3 (2.1%)	11.1 (2.4%)
Morocco	11.2	4.1
Ivory Coast	8.4	4.5
Sub-Saharan Africa[4]	58.9 (6.6%)	10.1 (2.2%)
Large East Asian Borrowers		
South Korea	48.0 (5.4%)	25.6 (5.5%)
Indonesia	35.8 (4.0%)	15.5 (3.3%)
Malaysia	18.0 (2.0%)	14.7 (3.2%)
Thailand	17.5 (2.0%)	7.5

[1]Includes long-term debt (original maturities more than one year), use of IMF credit, and short-term debt.
[2]Includes only long-term debt, combining public and publicly guaranteed debt to private creditors with private non-guaranteed debt.
[3]Includes several European countries: Portugal, Greece, Yugoslavia, Romania, and Hungary.
[4]Excludes Nigeria, Ivory Coast, and South Africa.

Source: World Bank, *World Debt Tables*, 1986-87 edition

when interest rates rose sharply in 1979-1981, these countries were highly exposed; and when financial confidence was lost and the supply of new lending dried up in 1982, they were immediately confronted with a severe cash flow problem. Finally, these Latin American nations and the other few "heavily indebted" countries have suffered a severe deterioration in economic performance since 1980 (Table 2). They are therefore a prime source of concern regarding possible domestic political backlash.

Sub-Saharan African Debt

The debt problems of sub-Saharan Africa have attracted much less attention than Latin American problems, and probably less than the region deserves.

Sub-Saharan Africa is comparable in population to Latin America, although much poorer. Its foreign debt is far smaller than Latin America's, but because of the poverty of the continent the indebtedness of many countries is considerably larger relative to GNP. (See Table 3.) The nature of this debt differs from Latin America's in ways that made the onset of debt problems less dramatic. Sub-Saharan Africa's debt is primarily long-term, fixed-interest debt owed to governments and international institutions; often the original interest rates were below market rates. The rise in world interest rates at the beginning of the 1980s was not immediately passed on to

TABLE 2

Real Per Capita GDP Growth, 1969-86
(annual changes, in percent)

	Average 1969-78[1]	1980	1981	1982	1983	1984	1985	1986
Western Hemisphere	3.3	3.1	−1.3	−3.2	−5.2	0.9	1.3	1.7
15 "heavily indebted"	3.6	2.6	−1.6	−2.7	−5.5	−0.1	0.9	1.4
Africa	2.2	0.6	−1.1	−2.2	−5.0	−1.4	−0.6	−1.2
Sub-Saharan Africa[2]	0.6	−0.2	−0.5	−2.2	−3.6	−0.8	1.0	0.9
Asia[3]	3.5	3.4	3.6	2.8	5.7	6.0	4.1	4.0

[1]Compound annual rate of exchange
[2]Excludes Nigeria and South Africa
[3]Prior to 1978, China not included. A regional breakdown for East Asian developing countries is not available.

Source: IMF, *World Economic Outlook*, April 1987, Table A6

TABLE 3

Long-Term and Short-Term External Debt[1]
Relative to GDP and to Exports, 1979-86: Groups of Countries
(in percent)

	1979	1980	1981	1982	1983	1984	1985	1986
Debt[2] to GDP								
Western Hemisphere	32.2	32.2	35.7	42.9	47.3	47.6	46.8	48.5
15 "heavily indebted"	30.2	30.8	34.6	41.7	47.0	46.8	46.3	48.4
Africa	30.6	27.2	31.4	37.5	39.8	40.3	44.9	49.2
Sub-Saharan Africa[3]	38.8	36.4	44.9	51.9	55.7	59.4	65.6	68.2
Asia[4]	16.7	17.2	19.1	22.1	23.4	24.0	27.2	29.6
Debt[2] to Exports								
Western Hemisphere	197.7	183.5	210.3	273.8	290.3	277.1	295.5	354.7
15 "heavily indebted"	182.3	167.1	201.4	269.8	289.7	272.1	284.2	337.9
Africa	107.1	90.2	116.3	153.8	170.4	170.1	181.0	219.6
Sub-Saharan Africa[3]	149.2	146.3	181.3	213.9	226.9	222.8	256.6	282.3
Asia[4]	75.7	71.9	74.5	88.4	93.6	88.1	100.0	101.6

[1]Excludes debt owed to IMF
[2]Year-end debt
[3]Excludes Nigeria and South Africa
[4]A regional breakdown for East Asian developing countries is not available.

Source: IMF, *World Economic Outlook,* April 1987, Table A50

the African nations, but instead has gradually filtered through in the form of rising charges on new borrowing and rescheduled debt. Because the creditors were official bodies, not private banks concerned about the risk of capital loss, there was no sudden cash flow crisis like that faced by the principal Latin American debtors in 1982. Furthermore, because sub-Saharan Africa's debt is relatively small and mostly not held by banks, African debt problems are not an important threat to world financial stability.

Nonetheless, the African debt problem has placed a growing burden on Africa's economies, contributing to the deterioration of an already unsatisfactory performance. With capital inflows from private sources dried up and net lending from official sources lower than in the past, African nations have been faced with balance-of-payments difficulties that have contributed to a decline in economic performance. At the same time, rescheduling of unpaid debt at market rates has contributed to a continuing growth of debt at rates that exceed economic growth, so that Africa's debt looks as if it is on an explosive and unsustainable path.

East Asia
Discussions of the debt problem usually focus on Latin America and Africa, because these are the areas where debt has become a crucial constraint on economic growth. East Asia, by contrast, has not so far suffered as greatly. Yet East Asian debt is large both in absolute terms and relative to the size of the economies. The two major East Asian debtors are Korea and Indonesia. Each has a foreign debt roughly comparable to Argentina's. The ratio of debt to GNP is comparable to that of Latin American debtors, and as in the Latin case, the debt is primarily bank loans at floating rates.

Given this surface similarity, the striking difference in experience is important. Unlike the Latin Americans, the East Asian debtors never suffered an interruption of normal access to capital markets, and have not been forced into austerity policies as severe as those adopted in Latin America. The East Asian case is thus an important control for assertions about the nature of the Latin problem.

B. THE 1983 DEBT STRATEGY FOR LATIN AMERICA

In 1982-83, under the pressure of events, the U.S. government, the International Monetary Fund, and the private creditors evolved an approach to managing the debt problems of the principal Latin American debtors. It will be helpful to have a shorthand way of referring to this approach: we will refer to the basic approach as the "1983 strategy," since it was in early 1983 that emergency crisis management gave way to a more or less coherent approach.

Situation in Early 1983
By early 1983 it was clear that the debt problems of developing countries were not simply the result of a short-term panic by banks, as some had at first maintained. For one thing, the debt crisis forced both countries and creditors to take stock of their situation, and this stock-taking revealed that developing country debt was larger than anyone had realized. Furthermore, the world economic picture had turned more adverse than anyone had previously believed possible. Real interest rates were at historic highs, and the purchasing power of many Third World exports was at its lowest point since the 1930s.

In the light of these developments, the debt crisis could not be viewed as just a problem brought on by banks' "herd instinct" that would pass when the shock was over. Banks now viewed the maximum debt that many countries could safely carry as less than what they had already borrowed. Thus, for at least several years, creditors would not willingly provide new lending or even roll over existing loans as they came due. On the other hand, if countries were to be suddenly obliged to service their debt entirely out of current income, the economic strain was widely regarded as insupportable. Thus, there was a perceived need for a way to avoid producing a rupture of relations between debtor countries and their creditors.

Elements of the Strategy

The debt strategy that emerged in 1983 had four main elements: rescheduling of existing debt, new lending by banks, additional financing by the IMF and other official institutions, and, as a *quid pro quo*, the imposition of stringent performance requirements on the debtor nations. We will discuss the rationale for this strategy in some detail later, but it is worth reviewing what the original plan envisaged.

The element of the strategy that was the source of the greatest concern in 1983 was the perceived need to mobilize banks to provide new lending. In order to reduce the burden of debt service to sustainable levels, it was believed that countries would have to not only reschedule all of their principal due but also be relent a substantial part of the interest. The lion's share of this new lending was expected to come from the private creditors themselves. This meant that banks would have to actually increase their claims on countries they perceived as highly risky. Typical estimates at the time were that banks should be expected to increase their exposure by 7 percent per year in nominal terms.

Even this new lending was expected, at least at first, to be inadequate. Thus private lending would be supplemented by public lending, from the IMF and to some extent other sources. This provision of official funds would actually serve several purposes: it would reduce somewhat the burden on the banks, it would be a "carrot" with which the IMF could mobilize the banks to do their part, and it would also help the IMF gain credibility for the final part of the strategy, the imposition of performance requirements on the debtor countries.

Essentially the debtor countries were to be placed under the standard framework of IMF conditionality. The IMF would serve as the agent of the creditors in requiring sound economic policies, notably exchange rate and budget adjustment, in principle ensuring that the provision of new lending helped resolve the debt problem instead of simply postponing the day of reckoning.

Assumptions of the Strategy

The 1983 debt strategy was based on four assumptions that represented a consensus view. It is useful to recall these assumptions in assessing whether a different strategy is now called for.

The first assumption was that countries simply could not pay the full interest due on their debt without new lending. The burden of such large payments was believed to be economically and certainly politically unbearable. Thus, new lending that covered at least a fraction of interest due was necessary.

Second, it was expected that private creditors could in fact be mobilized to provide most of the new lending, i.e., that the commercial banks could be persuaded (and to some extent arm-twisted) into increasing their exposure in developing countries.

Third, the architects of the 1983 strategy believed that if time could be bought with such emergency financing, the world economic environment facing debtors would improve dramatically. In particular, economic recovery in the industrial countries would raise the demand for developing country exports, while real interest rates would decline to historical levels.

Finally, it was believed that a combination of austerity and improving world conditions would restore the debtors to creditworthiness within a few years, allowing a resumption of voluntary lending and an end to the need for an officially imposed debt strategy.

C. THE AFRICAN DEBT STRATEGY

While most of the focus of both public attention and indeed of this report will be on the principal Latin American debtors, we should note that there has de facto also evolved a strategy for dealing with sub-Saharan African debt. This strategy differs in important respects from the Latin case, largely because of the difference in the initial situation.

The essential difference in the African case is the predominant role of official rather than private creditors. Because official lending is motivated largely by aid considerations rather than expected return, this lending did not cease as Latin lending did (although it has slowed, because even international agencies must worry to some extent about prospects for repayment). Furthermore, at least at first sub-Saharan African interest payments rose only slowly. The small private capital inflows into Africa did reverse. There has not, however, been an acute liquidity crisis in many countries.

Because interest payments did not rise as much, and because new lending continued, sub-Saharan Africa did not initially require a special mobilization of funds like that needed for Latin America. Instead, the financing problem could be met by the more conventional tool of rescheduling: postponement of the repayment of principal. This is a standard procedure in international finance. Rescheduling of official debt can be negotiated smoothly through established "Paris Club" procedures.

The problem has been that the magnitude and persistence of the rise in interest rates and the depression of African export prices have led to a gradual unraveling of the standard rescheduling solution. New debt has carried progressively higher interest rates; more important, rescheduling takes place at current market rates. Thus the interest burden on African nations has been rising steadily. In part this interest burden has been met by austerity programs that have contributed to a steady decline in per capita income; at the same time, countries have engaged in ever larger and more frequent rescheduling, and the growth of debt has begun to look explosive.

D. THE EVOLUTION OF
THE LATIN AMERICAN SITUATION, 1983-87

In one major sense the debt strategy adopted in 1983 has succeeded. There has not so far been a financial crisis, either a panic in the industrial countries or a unilateral decision by one or more major debtors to stop payment of debt service for more than a very short time. However, the assumptions on which that strategy was based have not been borne out. It is useful to examine each of the assumptions in turn.

Ability of Countries to Service Their Debt
One of the surprises of the period since 1983 has been the extraordinary ability of major debtors to turn their trade positions around. Brazil's trade deficit peaked at $2.8 billion in 1980, but was turned around to an extraordinary surplus of $13.1 billion by 1984. Mexico achieved a similar turnaround, from a $4.1 billion deficit in 1981 to a

$13.8 billion surplus in 1985; the collapse of oil prices, however, cut the surplus to less than $4 billion in 1986.

Willingness of Banks to Increase Exposure

If the ability of principal debtor countries to turn their trade positions around was a favorable surprise, it had its unfavorable counterpart in a failure of banks to undertake the expansion of exposure envisioned under the 1983 strategy. To understand what happened, it is necessary to distinguish between the major lending packages that banks have negotiated—the so-called concerted lending—and the various leakages that lead to net lending falling short of the amount lent in these jumbo packages.

Concerted lending was negotiated in two major rounds, in 1983 and 1984. In each case the banks undertook to lend a substantial part of the interest due. However, in a variety of ways banks—not necessarily the same banks making the jumbo loans—could attempt to reduce their exposure. To a limited extent this took the form of repayment of principal on the major loans; more important was contraction of trade credit lines and other forms of lending that were difficult to place under the specific agreements accompanying the jumbos. The effect was that bank capital flowed out the back door even as it was being made available at the front. In 1983, for example, financing packages to non-OPEC Latin America amounted to $10.5 billion, but the actual increase in bank exposure was only $3.6 billion. In 1984 the jumbo loans were almost completely matched by other reductions in exposure, so that the exposure of banks in Latin America actually fell slightly. In 1985 there was a small 2.7 percent increase in bank exposure in Latin America as parts of old packages continued to be disbursed, but this rate of exposure growth was far less than that envisaged under the original strategy.

The most recent (1986) Mexican package represents the first jumbo-type loan since 1984. It was negotiated *in extremis*, however; owing to the collapse in oil prices it was clear that unless something was done default was unavoidable. Thus it does not necessarily represent a resumption of the envisaged pattern of growing exposure.

The World Economic Environment

As expected in the original 1983 debt strategy, the industrial world did experience a substantial economic recovery in 1983-85 (although the growth was largely concentrated in North America and Japan, with Europe's performance remaining disappointing). While the recovery occurred, however, its effects on the economic position of debtor countries were disappointing in two respects. First, the anticipated recovery in commodity prices did not occur. Real commodity prices have remained at historically very low levels despite OECD recovery (Figure 1). This means, as we will argue at greater length below, that the burden of adjustment on commodity-exporting debtors attempting to service their debt has been high.

Second, while nominal interest rates have fallen, real interest rates (Figure 2) have remained much higher than during the 1970s (when they were particularly low) or even than during the 1950s and 1960s. For any given nominal interest rate, higher inflation makes it easier for a nation to reduce the ratio of debt to exports or GNP; thus the fact that interest rates have only fallen with the inflation rate has made more difficult than expected in 1983 a reduction of indicators of indebtedness and thus a restoration of the perception of creditworthiness.

FIGURE 1

Real Non-Oil Commodity Prices, 1957-87

(Index, 1956-86 = 100)

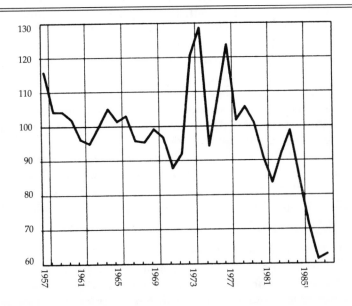

¹ Data after end-1986 are estimates.

Source: IMF, *World Economic Outlook*, April 1987, Chart 19

FIGURE 2

Real Interest Rates and LIBOR, 1975-86

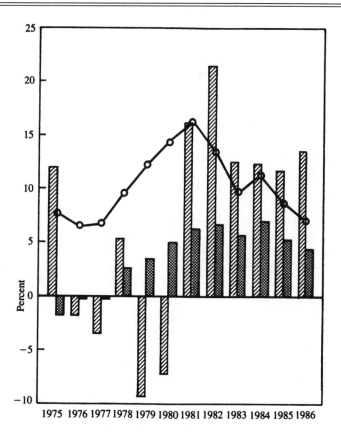

1975 1976 1977 1978 1979 1980 1981 1982 1983 1984 1985 1986

Real interest rate for: developing countries and the United States.
—o— Six-month dollar LIBOR.

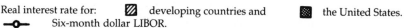

Note: The real interest rate is defined as the six-month dollar LIBOR deflated by the change in the export price index for developing countries. The U.S. real interest rate is defined as the six-month dollar LIBOR deflated by the U.S. GDP deflator.

Source: World Bank, *Developing Country Debt: Implementing the Consensus*, 1987, Figure Box 1

The reasons for the failure of OECD recovery to improve the environment of debtors are somewhat controversial. Among the important factors, however, we might mention the following. First, the persistence of the U.S. budget deficit has certainly helped keep real interest rates at abnormally high levels. Second, cautious monetary poli-cies, particularly in Western Europe (following Germany's lead), have both inhibited recovery and kept real interest rates high. Third, the debt crisis itself may have contributed to persistently low commodity prices. Faced with the necessity of increasing their earn-ings of foreign exchange, developing countries have tried to promote their exports, with commodities prominent among these. This kind of export promotion may have been somewhat counterproductive, be-cause it meant that prices of these goods were driven down on world markets.

Since early 1986 a new wild card has been thrown into the situa-tion by the sharp drop in the price of oil. This has mixed effects on the situation. Most particularly, it has opposite effects on the two largest debtors; Mexico's export revenues have been severely reduced while Brazil's import bill has been diminished.

Restoration of Normal Market Access

In part because of the failure of the external environment to improve, and perhaps also because of internal policy difficulties in the debtor countries (see below), the key objective of the 1983 strategy is still far from being achieved. Voluntary lending to principal Latin Amer-ican debtors has not resumed. Thus, any mitigation of the interest burden after principal is rescheduled will continue to have to come either from official lending or "involuntary" lending undertaken by current creditors in order to safeguard their outstanding exposure.

An imperfect but useful indicator of how far we are from restoring normal access to capital markets is the price for secondary market transactions in Latin American debt. The indicator is imperfect be-cause this is a thin market. Nonetheless, the size of the discounts at which the market places Latin debt is striking (Table 4). In Novem-ber 1986, claims on Mexico and Argentina were valued at only two-thirds of par, for instance. When the possibility of non-payment is regarded as this high, voluntary lending cannot be expected to re-sume, since a bank that lends a dollar to Mexico immediately finds itself with an asset worth only about 68 cents.

E. THE EFFECT OF THE DEBT PROBLEM ON GROWTH

We have argued that the central issue at this point is restoring growth in debtor nations. It is therefore important to look again at the growth performance of heavily indebted developing countries

TABLE 4

Secondary Market Prices of Developing Country Debt, November 1986
(percent of par)

Argentina	65.7
Bolivia	7.5
Chile	75.5
Mexico	68.0
Philippines	73.0
Venezuela	74.5

Source: Salomon Brothers

1980 (Table 2). The basic point is that countries that recorded fairly rapid growth and steadily rising output per capita in the 1970s have now experienced a prolonged period of declining or stagnant per capita GNP.

F. THE OUTLOOK IN 1987

Perhaps the best way to view the current state of the debt problem is to compare it with two reference points: the actual situation in 1983, when the basic debt strategy was set in motion, and the position that the creators of the debt strategy expected to have achieved by now.

The current situation is better than that of early 1983 in several respects. While the terms of trade of debtor countries are not much better than they were, despite OECD recovery, the decline in real interest rates from their peak has been significant, even if not as great as hoped. Further, the remarkable turnaround of trade performance in several debtor countries shows that their economies are surprisingly resilient.

On the other hand, the current situation is not nearly as good as that which many observers in 1983 widely expected would prevail by now. The external environment facing debtors has not experienced the substantial improvement that was a key assumption of the 1983 debt strategy. Most important, neither normal access to capital markets nor sustained economic growth has been restored.

Perhaps the most important difference between 1983 and 1987 is that of the forward-looking outlook. In 1983 the immediate situation was very difficult, but the difficulty was widely regarded as temporary. Since economic recovery, declining real interest rates and restoration of access to capital markets were regarded as likely to improve the position of debtors substantially in the medium term, it made sense to pursue a debt strategy that was in large part one of buying time. In 1987, by contrast, the prospects for an autonomous improvement in the situation are much less apparent. Real interest rates could fall, commodity prices could rise, and so on; oil prices in particular are likely to rise well above their 1986 trough. In general, however, there is no longer a presumption that things will get much better of their own accord. New additional funds are clearly needed to reduce the near-term burden of paying interest on the existing debt. More generally, in the face of rising interest rates and deteriorating economic growth, we need to reconsider the underlying logic of the 1983 debt strategy, and ask whether a different strategy will be appropriate in the future.

II. Conceptual Issues

Before proceeding to a discussion of debt strategy innovations, it is important to clarify key conceptual issues. A conceptual framework for thinking about debt is essential. Three issues in particular need to be brought out—all three often misunderstood.

First, the burden on the debtor country is best measured by the net resource transfer in or out of the country in the period in question—a quite different measure from that of growth of indebtedness. An essential point to keep in mind is that since 1982, even while debt has continued to grow, resource transfer from developed countries to debtors has reversed and actually become a large resource transfer back to creditors.

Second, we need to discuss the macroeconomic aspects of resource transfer to understand the problems posed for economic growth in the debtor countries. The point is that making outward resource transfers on the scale that highly indebted countries have made them since 1983 puts serious strains on any economy. In the developing countries the main consequences of this strain have been a sharp decline in growth, large declines in real wages, and persistent problems with inflation. These adverse consequences could be avoided and adequate growth achieved by limiting the magnitude of the resource transfers.

Finally, we need to discuss the financial issues facing creditors. The central issue here is the elusive distinction between liquidity and solvency problems: when does it make sense to stretch out payments to buy time; when does it make sense to write off debt and possibly reduce a debtor's obligations?

A. BORROWING, INDEBTEDNESS, AND RESOURCE TRANSFERS

The problem of coping with the debt overhang is perhaps best viewed as a tension between two goals. On one hand, creditors view the current level of debt as risky because it is too large relative to the debtor countries' ability to service it. They therefore want to see countries reducing their debt burdens as rapidly as possible. On the other hand, the debtor countries want to maintain economic growth and rising living standards. This will be easier, the less the burden of payment on the debt. These goals conflict, so the problem is one of striking a balance acceptable to both sides.

As a way to think about the tradeoff between resource transfer and debt growth, it is useful to begin with a simplified numerical example.

A Numerical Example

Let's imagine a roughly Brazil-sized country. It will be assumed to have a GNP of $200 billion and a foreign debt of half that, around $100 billion, on which it pays an average interest rate of 9 percent. The domestic economy has a long-run growth rate of 4 percent per year, and the dollar prices of the country's exports are rising at 3 percent per year.

Suppose that this economy has rescheduled all of the principal due on its debt, and further is able to obtain $3 billion in new money from its creditors, whose exposure therefore grows by 3 percent per year. How are we to evaluate the country's position vis-à-vis its own goals and those of its creditors?

A crude view would focus only on the fact that the country is getting deeper into debt. This view would conclude that creditors are throwing good money after bad, and that the country is getting away with a free ride. Yet this view would be wrong on both counts.

First, although the country's debt in dollar terms is growing, its indebtedness relative to its ability to repay is falling. Ultimately a country's ability to service debt depends on its ability to produce goods and services. In our example, the gross national product is rising by 4 percent per year, while world prices are rising an additional 3 percent per year. Thus the value of the country's output is rising 7 percent per year, compared with only a 3 percent annual rise in debt. So the ratio of debt to GNP, i.e. the ratio of debt to the country's ability to repay, actually declines 4 percent per year.

Second, the country is hardly getting a free ride. In the first year it must pay $9 billion in interest, while receiving only $3 billion in new money. The additional $6 billion—3 percent of GNP—must be paid for by exporting more than the country imports. The resources used to produce these extra exports are in effect made available to creditor countries for their consumption and investment, rather than being available for domestic use. Thus the country is making a resource transfer to the rest of the world each year of 3 percent of its GNP.

Notice that what we are here calling resource transfer is also the excess of the exports of a country over its imports—that is, its trade surplus (where trade includes services other than interest payments). It is useful to call this surplus a resource transfer, however, because this term emphasizes the point that it is a burden, not an advantage, for the debtor country. It is all too easy to fall into a mercantilist view in which a country that runs large trade surpluses is believed to be somehow benefiting from the exchange. For a debtor nation a trade surplus is not something it gets away with; it is something it has to achieve to service its debt.

Clearly a debtor country could avoid the burden of making a resource transfer by failing to honor its debt. There are strong reasons why countries do not do this, but pointing out this fact reminds us that the net resource transfer rather than the level of borrowing is the correct measure of the burden of debt on a country in any particular period.

Now some level of outward resource transfers is not necessarily a bad thing when the current level of debt is excessive. Indeed, as long as the interest rate exceeds the rate of growth some outward resource transfer is necessary to prevent debt from growing faster than the ability to repay. In our example, if there were no resource transfer— if the country borrowed all of its interest—debt would grow at 9 percent, two percent faster than the GNP. This would be unacceptable if the creditor felt that the original debt level was already excessive. On the other hand, if creditors were to insist on full payment of interest without new lending, the necessary resource transfer of $9 billion would be 4.5 percent of GNP, a very large number. If the creditors insisted on some net repayment of principal, the required resource transfer would be even larger.

The example strongly suggests that if there is a middle ground in which the outward resource transfer is tolerable from the point of view of the debtor nation, yet indebtedness falls fast enough relative to repayment capacity to satisfy creditors, it is likely to involve a rising nominal value of debt over time. It is also clear from this example that the appropriate amount of new money will differ from country to country depending on the particular circumstances of that country.

Debt and Resource Transfer since 1982

With the cutoff of normal access to the capital markets for many debtor nations in 1982, the direction of resource transfer suddenly reversed. In 1981 there was a large net inward resource transfer to the major LDC debtors. This resource transfer was sharply cut in 1982, and since then has run strongly the other way. Thus, from the point of view of the debtors, the debt problem required and was met by a major adjustment of their external balances. (Table 5 indicates net resource transfers and growth of indebtedness for three groups of countries.)

Was this shift to net outward resource transfers enough to reduce the rate of growth of debt below that of the eventual capacity to service debt? At first glance the results are not encouraging. As Table 3

TABLE 5

Resource Transfers and Net Borrowing, 1980-85
(US$ billions)

	1980	1981	1982	1983	1984	1985
15 Highly-Indebted Countries						
A. Increase in net indebtedness (current account deficit)	29.5	50.3	50.6	15.2	0.6	0.1
B. Net investment income (interest, profits, etc.)	−16.7	−26.1	−37.8	−36.2	−38.9	−37.5
C. Resource transfer (A + B)	12.8	24.2	12.8	−21.0	−38.3	−37.4
D. Resource transfer as % of GNP	1.5	2.5	1.4	−2.5	−4.4	−4.2
Western Hemisphere						
A. Increase in net indebtedness (current account deficit)	30.2	42.7	42.4	10.9	2.6	4.7
B. Net investment income (interest, profits, etc.)	−15.9	−24.3	−34.3	−32.6	−34.7	−33.0
C. Resource transfer (A + B)	14.3	18.1	8.1	−21.7	−32.1	−28.3
D. Resource transfer as % of GNP	2.0	2.3	1.0	−3.0	−4.2	−3.6
Sub-Saharan Africa						
A. Increase in net indebtedness (current account deficit)	8.4	9.9	8.6	5.9	3.5	3.3
B. Net investment income (interest, profits, etc.)	−2.2	−2.4	−2.7	−2.7	−3.3	−3.4
C. Resource transfer (A + B)	6.2	7.5	5.9	3.2	0.2	−0.1
D. Resource transfer as % of GNP	5.2	6.9	5.7	3.2	0.2	−0.1

above shows, the ratio of debt to GNP has remained roughly constant since 1983 for the "heavily indebted" countries (and rose for sub-Saharan Africa), while the ratio of debt to exports, another widely used indicator, rose for both groups. (Table 6 shows some of the variation among individual countries.) However, these indicators are

TABLE 6

Total External Debt Relative to GNP and to Exports of Goods and Services, 1980-85: Individual Countries
(in percent)

	1980	1981	1982	1983	1984	1985
Debt to GNP						
Brazil	29.0	30.3	34.0	49.8	52.4	51.3
Mexico	31.9	34.0	55.5	69.8	60.4	58.3
Argentina	51.1	65.6	79.9	75.5	64.4	79.9
Venezuela	50.2	48.4	48.0	49.4	70.2	66.0
Chile	45.5	50.3	77.9	100.4	115.1	142.2
Philippines	49.6	54.2	61.9	70.5	76.2	80.6
Nigeria	10.3	15.6	16.9	24.4	25.2	25.7
Zambia	90.2	92.0	100.1	118.7	154.5	210.3
Sudan	67.3	67.1	78.5	91.6	92.3	79.9
Mali	43.3	58.9	69.7	91.4	119.8	129.5
South Korea	49.3	50.4	54.4	53.8	52.5	57.7
Indonesia	27.9	25.4	29.4	39.0	37.6	44.9
Debt to Exports						
Brazil	301.6	296.3	388.7	401.6	342.1	365.1
Mexico	233.2	257.5	310.6	324.6	300.0	327.6
Argentina	242.5	301.6	448.7	461.9	474.0	467.8
Venezuela	133.1	130.2	158.2	186.0	173.5	191.8
Chile	193.1	279.7	336.6	376.8	414.6	430.4
Philippines	218.3	242.8	303.8	295.7	305.9	330.1
Nigeria	32.0	61.2	96.6	165.6	147.3	141.2
Zambia	199.6	306.9	338.2	364.7	403.2	529.3
Sudan	454.1	455.3	683.6	832.5	845.6	759.7
Mali	277.1	411.4	459.6	482.9	548.5	681.8
South Korea	131.8	122.1	133.1	134.5	128.3	145.2
Indonesia	94.1	91.2	124.6	151.4	146.5	178.7

Source: World Bank, *World Debt Tables*, 1986-87 edition

distorted by short-run effects. Export growth was depressed by the continuing slump in world commodity prices, a trend unlikely to continue. Output growth in Latin America was depressed well below its long-run level by recessions induced by the need to make the outward resource transfer itself. Moreover, the real depreciation of the debtor country currencies relative to the dollar automatically increased the ratio of the debt measured in dollars to the country's exports. In a longer-term perspective, rates of resource transfer as large as we have seen should in fact be more than large enough to improve the relevant ratios; the question is instead what rate of resource transfer is actually sustainable over the medium and longer term in each country.

The African case is different. Resource transfer remained inward in direction until 1984, and turned strongly outward only in 1985. Meanwhile the rate of growth of Africa's economies was even lower than in Latin America. As a result, Africa's debt grew significantly faster than its output, with less reason than in Latin America's case to believe that the depression of growth would be only temporary. While the scenario in which an acceptable rate of resource transfer keeps the debt from growing as fast as the capacity to service it is plausible for Latin America, it does not look reasonable for Africa.

B. RESOURCE TRANSFER AND ECONOMIC GROWTH

We come now to the key problem of the debtor countries: outward resource transfer above some critical level for each country makes it very difficult for that country to achieve adequate economic growth. Inevitably, an outward resource transfer requires either a cut in domestic consumption, reduced investment, or both. In practice, an excessively large resource transfer almost invariably leads to large scale unemployment of domestic labor and capital, multiplying the impact on both the standard of living and the prospects for future growth. The key problem therefore is to identify a rate of resource transfer that is consistent with desirable economic growth but that also shrinks the debt relative to the country's long-run ability to pay.

Methods for Achieving Resource Transfer
As we have already noted, resource transfer must be achieved either through increased exports or reduced imports. In order to achieve such changes in trade flows, countries have at their disposal two

broad types of policy: expenditure-reducing and expenditure-switching.

An expenditure-reducing program attempts to improve the trade balance by reducing expenditure, so that domestic demand falls. Examples of expenditure-reducing policies are tax increases, budget cuts, and credit tightening. These policies will have a direct impact on demand for imports, since some of the reduction in demand will be a reduction in demand for imported goods. They may also have a direct effect on exports, to the extent that domestic demand competes with export demand for domestic goods. For example, suppose that the government of Argentina is able to enforce a decline in consumer spending. This will directly reduce imports of consumer durables and other consumption goods that Argentina buys from abroad. It may also increase beef exports, because Argentine consumers will purchase less beef, releasing more for the export market.

The other method for achieving resource transfer is to switch expenditures from foreign onto domestic goods. This may involve either shifting demand of domestic residents from imports to domestic products, or promoting exports by inducing foreigners to buy more domestic goods. Examples of expenditure-switching policies are currency devaluation, import controls, and export subsidies.

It is a standard proposition of international economic analysis that a program to achieve outward resource transfer should include both expenditure-reducing and expenditure-switching measures. An expenditure-reduction program, on its own, is a very costly way to improve the trade balance. Only part of the reduction in demand will come at the expense of imports or goods that can be exported. The rest of the demand reduction will come at the expense of domestic goods, and will be reflected in a decline in output, capacity utilization, and employment.

On the other hand, a program that relies only on expenditure switching cannot succeed unless there are already substantial unemployed resources in the economy. Otherwise, when demand is switched from foreign to domestic products, the result will be an excess demand for domestic resources that leads to inflation, which dissipates the intended gains.

Ideally, a country could fine-tune a program that combined expenditure switching and expenditure reduction so as to achieve a move to outward resource transfer without a fall in domestic output or a rise in unemployment. In practice, however, debtor countries that have been forced to move quickly into large net resource transfers have relied heavily on expenditure reduction and, as a result, have suffered deep recessions. But over a longer time horizon, a debtor country can make substantial outward resource transfers while maintaining healthy economic growth.

Problems of Resource Transfer

The reasons why achieving resource transfer is so expensive in practice are fairly clear. In order to pursue expenditure-switching policies, countries must raise the prices of foreign goods relative to those of domestically produced goods. This is true whether the tool is devaluation or import quotas; indeed import quotas usually raise prices even more than devaluation.

The immediate result is a decline in real wages, especially of workers in protected industries selling to the domestic market. Mexico is a case in point: real wages of manufacturing workers, mostly in the protected import-substituting industries, have fallen some 40 percent since their 1981 peak—far more than the decline in overall per capita real income in Mexico in the same period. This fall in real wages is likely to pose significant political and social problems. Equally serious, explicit or implicit indexation of wages can easily convert a devaluation or other expenditure-switching policy into an inflationary spiral. If wages rise to compensate for the effects of the devaluation, the expenditure-switching effects of the devaluation will be eroded, forcing another devaluation, and so on.

The experience of Brazil in 1986 illustrates the point. Brazil shifted from a policy based on achieving resource transfer largely through expenditure reduction to an expenditure-switching policy built around a steep devaluation of the cruzeiro. The initial effects were highly favorable: the trade balance continued to improve and growth picked up to a remarkable 8 percent. However, inflationary pressures quickly mounted, with the inflation rate rising to 238 percent at the beginning of 1987.

The perception of this difficulty has led debtor countries sooner or later to be cautious with their devaluations, supplementing them with very severe programs of expenditure reduction. These expenditure reduction programs have brought in their wake sharp declines in economic growth, to such an extent that the secondary cost of the decline in economic growth has been substantially larger than the direct cost of the resource transfer.

The Relation Between Resource Transfer and Growth

It is clear from the preceding discussion that an increase in the level of the outward resource transfer required of a country will temporarily reduce its economic growth, and conversely that a reduction in this burden may be expected to allow temporarily faster growth. It should also be clear, however, that there is not a simple mechanical relationship between the level of resource transfer and the rate of economic growth. It depends on the extent to which the resource transfer can be achieved via expenditure switching rather than expenditure reduction. Experience has shown that it is in practice necessary that a substantial part of the temporary burden be borne by expenditure reduction, and thus that a large price be paid.

To get some idea of the possible size of this price, suppose that a country has a marginal propensity to import of 0.2; that is, of a dollar of spending reduction, one-fifth falls on imports and the rest on domestic goods. For this country to achieve a resource transfer of 3 percent of GNP through expenditure cutting alone would require that total demand be reduced by 15 percent, and thus that demand for domestic goods fall by 12 percent. The result would be a 12 percent fall in domestic output; this would be a secondary burden four times as large as the direct cost of making the resource transfer.

If some expenditure switching is possible, the burden can be reduced. In this example, however, even if the size of the domestic output reduction could be cut in half, to 6 percent, the secondary consequence of the resource transfer for economic growth would still be twice as large as the resource transfer itself.

It should be emphasized, however, that this is only a short-run effect of *increasing* the resource transfer. In the medium term, a substantial resource transfer *is* consistent with healthy economic growth. For example, the government of Brazil has recently estimated that a resource transfer of 2.5 percent of gross national product would be consistent with future real GNP growth at a 7 percent annual rate.

Budget Deficits and Inflation

We have stressed the link between expenditure-switching policies and inflation in debtor countries. It should be noted, however, that another potent source of inflation is the problem of budget deficits. A country with an intractable budget deficit can develop severe inflation problems for purely internal reasons, though these problems usually interact with its debt difficulties.

The problem develops when a country cannot finance its budget deficit except by printing money. (This is of course a condition more likely to occur when foreign borrowing has become impossible.) When governments rely on monetary financing of their deficits beyond low levels, inflation can quickly soar to hyperinflation levels. The reason is that a vicious circle sets in. As the public comes to expect high inflation, it economizes on the use of money by making more frequent transactions and finding substitutes (such as foreign currency). As the real value of the money in circulation falls, however, the government is forced to expand the stock in circulation at an accelerating rate in order to achieve the same real revenue—and this leads to accelerated inflation and even a further decline in the use of money. In recent years Argentina, Brazil, and Israel have all seen inflation quickly spiral into hundreds of percent per year, and Bolivia had a true hyperinflation with an annual 40,000 percent price increase.

A necessary precondition for bringing such budget-driven inflations under control is to correct the budget, raising taxes and cutting expenditure to the point where the government's needs can be met without money issue. Even when this is done, however, governments have usually relied on other measures as well. Most notably, these have included pegging the exchange rate, introducing new currencies, and imposing temporary wage-price controls.

There may in many instances be a good case for these measures. High inflation tends to become an inertial process, with expectations of inflation driving the inflationary process itself. It makes sense to use easily visible signals, such as an exchange rate freeze or a price freeze, to dramatize the change in regime and bring inflation to a rapid halt; otherwise, controlling inflation will probably require a prolonged, severe recession. However, for a debtor country the goal of controlling inflation is likely to conflict with the need to make large resource transfers to creditors. An exchange rate freeze helps throw cold water on inflationary expectations, but it also conflicts with attempts to achieve large trade surpluses. Wage and price controls can help break the wage-price spiral, but they demand a political consensus that may have to be bought with concessions that undermine the effort to hold imports down and promote exports.

The problem of budget deficits and inflation, then, while its origins may lie in domestic issues rather than international debt, interacts with the problem of achieving resource transfer in a way that complicates an already difficult task.

Capital Flight

The issue of capital flight represents both a cause and a symptom of the international debt problem. Avoiding unwanted outward resource transfers and limiting the needed amounts of external credits requires debtor countries to find ways to reduce capital flight and to induce the repatriation of previous flight capital.

The initiatives to induce capital repatriation might include amnesty for capital previously transferred abroad illegally, tax concessions for repatriated capital, an exchange of assets held abroad for government bonds denominated in foreign currencies, etc. A more fundamental precondition for facilitating the return of flight capital is to restore confidence in the national economy by establishing a favorable investment environment at home through such things as privatization of inefficient state-owned enterprises and the maintenance of realistic interest and exchange rate levels.

An important prerequisite for securing inflows of fresh capital from abroad is undoubtedly to convince foreign investors in general, and commercial banks in particular, that their money will be used in a productive way. In particular, it is important for both the lenders and the debtor countries to avoid so-called round-tripping, in which new funds escape through increased investment outflows. Governments must exercise control to avoid such round-tripping in the context of debt-equity swaps.

C. LIQUIDITY AND SOLVENCY PROBLEMS

We have now seen two main points. First, from the point of view of creditors it is essential that countries achieve a sufficiently large resource transfer that their debt grows more slowly than their carrying capacity, as measured, say, by GNP. Second, from the point of view of debtor countries the resource transfer must be limited in magnitude if the debtor is to achieve a satisfactory rate of economic growth and limit the resources used to service debt rather than for domestic investment or consumption.

The conflict between these objectives defines the key issue of whether the debt problem is one of liquidity or solvency. Without attempting any exact definition, we would define the problem to be one of "liquidity" if a combination of rescheduling and new money could plausibly provide the bridge to a future restoration of normal access to markets, while we would define it as one of "solvency" if this does not look possible.

Assessing Liquidity Versus Solvency

The problem may be stated as follows: is a sustainable level of resource transfer enough to reduce the ratio of debt to GNP significantly over time? If so, then the problem is one of inducing enough relending of interest to reduce resource transfer to this acceptable level. The main difficulty is one of mobilizing funds, and the main risk is that a failure to mobilize funds will impose an unacceptable burden on the debtor and thus force an unnecessary rupture of relations between debtor and creditors. This was the view taken at the inception of the 1983 debt strategy.

On the other hand, suppose that the maximum level of resource transfer that seems possible, either economically or politically, is not enough to prevent the growth of debt from outpacing economic growth in both the near term and the more distant future. Then the problem is one of solvency. In this case it is necessary to look for some international equivalent of a bankruptcy proceeding.

For the major Latin American debtors it is still possible to make a case that the problem is one of liquidity, not solvency. The rates of resource transfer achieved by Mexico and Brazil in 1984 were clearly too high to be politically sustainable over the long term. However, the fact that they were achieved even briefly indicates the ability of these economies to generate substantial surpluses on their trade accounts. Moreover, if sustained growth in these economies can be resumed, such a large resource transfer should not be needed. For both countries a long-term growth rate of 4-5 percent, not much less than the current level of real interest rates, seems reasonable. This would seem to imply that net resource transfers of 2 or so percent of GNP should be enough to steadily reduce debt to GNP ratios. The problem is then one of finding a mechanism that allows the debt to grow in dollar terms fast enough to allow this acceptable level of resource transfer.

By contrast, the African situation does not look like a liquidity problem. By comparison with the Latin case, the outward resource transfer has come late and been of modest extent, yet the growth performance has been quite literally disastrous. As we saw, the extent of resource transfer has been insufficient to prevent what looks like a runaway growth in debt. Thus, it is hard to see how to regard the African debt problem as other than one of basic solvency.

Defensive Lending When the Problem is One of Liquidity

Suppose that we conclude that the problem of a debtor country is one of liquidity, not solvency. This immediately raises an objection: if this is the case, why are private lenders not willing to solve the problem? That is, if a country will be able to pay its way eventually, why isn't it profitable for banks or other investors to lend it the money to get through its current difficulties, without need for special negotiations, the intervention of the IMF, and so on?

The answer to this question requires that we recognize, first, that the line between liquidity and solvency is not a sharp boundary. A country experiencing a liquidity problem is necessarily one where there is a significant perceived risk of a failure to repay—if there is no such risk, the country will be able to borrow freely, and it will not have a liquidity problem. The difference between a liquidity problem and a solvency problem is that in the case of a liquidity problem the risk of nonpayment is only a probability, not the most likely outcome.

As long as there is a significant risk of non-payment, however, new lenders will not voluntarily provide money to a country at a rate of interest that is consistent with a declining ratio of debt to GNP. Thus, the fact that Mexican bonds trade at an implicit interest rate of nearly 15 percent in the secondary market suggests that Mexico could not both service its debt and grow if it had to pay the full implicit market rate on its external debt. But with the below-market rate now charged on new lending to Mexico, Mexico can support economic growth at a rate that is faster than the rate of growth of its external debt and thus reduce its ratio of debt to GNP and to exports.

A liquidity problem can generate a crisis: a country, unable to borrow, finds that in order to avoid default it must service its debt fully out of current income. This implies an unacceptably large resource transfer; and thus the country may be forced by domestic politics into a premature and unnecessary default.

In this situation it makes sense for a country's creditors to engage in defensive lending to preserve their position. That is, by engaging in new lending, even though there is a risk that they will not be fully repaid for the additional money they lend, they enhance the probability of repayment on existing debt enough to make the acceptance of additional exposure worthwhile.

An example may make the case for such defensive lending clear. Suppose that a country's creditors believe that if they do not engage in defensive lending, the liquidity problems of a country will force a default and they will realize only 60 cents on each dollar of obligations. On the other hand, they believe that by lending the country enough additional money, they can reduce the risk of default to the point that the expected capital loss is only 20 cents. In this situation the prospect of lending new money is hardly attractive: viewed in isolation the additional lending incurs a 20 percent capital loss. But it has the benefit of raising the expected value of outstanding debt.

How much additional exposure should the creditors be willing to accept? Each dollar of additional exposure represents 20 cents of loss, but the lending package adds 20 cents to the value of each dollar of existing claims. Thus, from the point of view of the creditors as a group, a program of defensive lending would be worth undertaking as long as the new lending was less than the existing claims. At maximum, they should be willing to double their exposure! For the sake of comparison, the increase in bank exposure in Latin America from the end of 1982 to the end of 1985 was only 6 percent.

The Problem of Coordination

Given that there is a case for defensive lending in the face of a liquidity problem, it may still be unclear why this is a problem of public policy. Why can't creditors simply act in their own interest?

To understand this, we need to distinguish between the collective interest of creditors and the interest of each individual creditor. The case for defensive lending rests on the point that the overall lending of a country's creditors raises the value of all their claims on the country. For each individual creditor, however, the effect of its own actions on the value of its claims on the country will usually be quite small. Suppose that an individual creditor owns 5 percent of a country's debt. Then even if that creditor is willing to double its exposure, this will amount to only a 5 percent increase in the country's debt, probably not enough to make much difference in the country's ability to continue debt service. So if this bank acts alone in trying to defend the value of its claims, it will accept large risks for little purpose.

Thus, from the point of view of each creditor acting independently, it does not usually make sense to engage in defensive lending. Instead, each creditor has an incentive to extract itself as best as it can, demanding full payment wherever possible and refusing to make new loans that draw it deeper into the situation.

The problem is that if each creditor does this, the result will be precisely to force the liquidity crisis that it is in the creditors' collective interest to avoid.

Now, in practice the situation is not this bad. There are usually several larger creditors that are large enough to act in a somewhat coordinated fashion. Nonetheless, the problem of coordination bedevils any debt strategy that relies on growing debt despite a perceived risk that debt will not be repaid in full.

The answer of the 1983 strategy was to supplement the independent actions of the creditors in two ways. First, the IMF and central banks actively tried to lean on the banks to act in their collective self-interest, using moral suasion to induce "involuntary" (so-called coordinated) new lending. Second, private defensive lending was supplemented by official money: IMF and other official lending was to take on a significant part of the burden of reducing the required resource transfer to manageable levels.

Does It Ever Make Sense to Forgive Debt?

The logic of the case for defensive lending, carried to its extreme, suggests that a country's debt need never be forgiven. As long as there is some chance that a country's ability to repay may suddenly increase—through a mineral discovery, for example—creditors could just keep relending enough of the interest to keep resource transfer within acceptable bounds.

There are several reasons not to push the argument to this logical extreme. First, the process of recycling interest is not costless; on the contrary, negotiations between banks and creditors are extremely wearing, distracting both governments and banks from attending to their normal business. Second, the presence of an overhang of debt unlikely to be repaid interferes with normal business, which relies on extensive use of explicit and implicit credit. A supplier, for example, will be reluctant to extend credit when an overnight loan may find itself converted into a 30-year claim, valued at 40 percent of par.

Finally, a large debt overhang that nobody expects will ever be fully paid or serviced at market interest rates undermines the incentive for responsible action on the part of the debtor. Why should a debtor make strong efforts to promote exports or substitute for imports when any gain will be claimed by the creditors? If creditors demand the maximum resource transfer the country can manage, and they will do so forever, then there is no reason for the country to do anything to make its ability to generate resources larger.

For all these reasons, in an extreme case where the possibility of ever restoring normal access to capital markets is sufficiently remote, it might make sense to forgive part of the debt. In principle, such forgiveness could actually raise the value of creditors' claims. If the present value of a country's obligations is reduced by 30 percent, but the chance of repayment is 95 percent, this is worth more to creditors than debt claimed at full value but with only a 50 percent chance of being honored.

One serious problem in such a case, of course, is how to offer debt forgiveness while setting limits. If 30 percent of debt can be forgiven, why not 50 or 75 percent? Unfortunately, there is no legal structure for sovereign debt that establishes guidelines once the initial terms of a debt contract have been breached. Moreover, there is the further problem of how to offer such debt relief to one country without creating overwhelming political pressures in other countries for debt relief or a unilateral moratorium.

III. Broader Interests

A. THE INTERESTS OF CREDITOR NATIONS

The preceding discussion of liquidity and solvency focuses on the narrowly financial interest of creditors in minimizing the loss in value of their claims on problem debtors. Such a narrow focus is useful as a way of isolating some key arguments. Clearly, however, this is not the whole of either the actual or the appropriate interest of creditors. This is especially true when we turn from the interests of private creditor institutions to those of multilateral agencies and creditor country governments. Thus we turn next to some broader interests of the creditors.

Safeguarding the Financial System

One important reason for concern about the debt problem is that losses by banks can have larger consequences than losses to individual bondholders. The reason is the role of banks as financial intermediaries. This role means both that banks are highly leveraged, with their net worth much less than their assets, and that insolvency by major banks could disrupt the working of the financial system.

The key point is that although bank claims on problem debtors are only a small fraction of the wealth of the industrial countries, in aggregate they considerably exceed the net worth of the banks. Some illustrative numbers are provided in Table 7. These numbers show that if the problem debtors were to repudiate all or most of their debt, the effect could be to put a number of major Trilateral banks out of business. This in turn could disrupt the normal functioning of financial markets. If the monetary authorities of the industrial countries were to remain passive in the face of these disruptions, the result could be a severe monetary contraction reminiscent of the early 1930s.

While the risk posed by debt to the international financial system is a significant feature of the situation, however, it should not be exaggerated. First, the likelihood that debt would actually place the banking system in jeopardy is small, since a near-total repudiation of debt is extremely unlikely. Furthermore, the capital of major

TABLE 7

Exposure of Commercial Banks

	Latin American Loans (US$ billions)	as % of total equity	reserves as % of exposure
American			
Citicorp	11.6	80	25
Bank of America	7.3	178	29
Chase Manhattan	7.0	190	15
Morgan Guaranty	4.6	88	20
Chemical	5.3	168	20
Manufacturers			
Hanover	7.6	202	13
British			
Barclays	4.0	65	7
Lloyds	8.7	193	7
Midland	7.1	210	8
National Westminster	4.2	54	13
	Loans to 31 Developing Countries		
Japanese			
The Bank of Tokyo	5.2	128.3	>5
Dai-Ichi Kangyo	3.4	57	>5
Fuji Bank	2.6	41.2	>5
Industrial Bank of			
Japan	2.6	57.5	>5
West German			
Deutsche	3.4	40	70
Commerzbank	3.2	115	na
Dresdner	3.4	na	50
Swiss			
Crédit Suisse	1.6	39	>30
Swiss Bank Corp.	2.1	35	>30
Union Bank of			
Switzerland	2.4	40	>30

Note: Great caution must be taken in interpreting this table given differences across nations in the accounting of bank assets and capital. Definitions of capital vary as do practices for setting aside reserves.

Source: *The Economist* (May 30, 1987), p. 77. Other sources used by the *Economist* include Salomon Bros., Keefe Bruyette & Woods, and IBCA.

banks has been growing much more rapidly than their Latin American exposure, so that the risk of bank insolvency due to a debt crisis has been receding. (Table 8 indicates this for major U.S. banks. For banks in Japan and Europe, the large decline in the U.S. dollar—in which most debt is still denominated—is an added factor helping to diminish exposure relative to capital and reserves.) Moreover, even if the debt crisis should lead to bank insolvency, the monetary authorities have sufficient instruments available to keep the banking system operating, and are both able and willing to supply enough liquidity to prevent a debt repudiation from leading to a depression.

It is worth keeping in mind that, fundamentally, international debt is not large relative to the world economy. The claims of banks on problem debtors represent about one percent of the assets of the industrialized countries, and the income from these claims is about 0.25 percent of OECD GNP. Even if a large fraction of the debt should have to be written off, there is no fundamental reason why the consequences to the creditor nations need be severe.

Trade/Finance Linkages

The consequences of debt problems for the industrial countries of course go beyond the banking system. The rapid shift of debtor nations into trade surplus after 1981 had as its counterpart a sharp fall in industrial country exports to these countries, and to a lesser extent a rise in debtor exports to the OECD countries. These associated trade shifts were particularly painful for the United States, with a rapidly deteriorating overall trade balance at the same time and

TABLE 8

Exposure of Nine Largest U.S. Banks
(claims as % of capital, end of year)

	1982	1985
All Developing Countries	284.0	191.8
Latin American Countries	176.5	129.2
Brazil	48.8	39.3
Mexico	45.2	34.2
Venezuela	26.2	17.4
Argentina	19.1	14.6

Source: United Nations Conference on Trade and Development, *Trade and Development Report, 1986,* Annex table 22

with the largest trading relationship with Latin America among Trilateral countries. Especially in America, this trade/finance linkage is often cited as a reason for official concern with the debt problem.

This issue is often stated as a simple one of employment: lost exports to developing countries cost jobs in the industrial nations. To put the issue this way is however to oversimplify. The overall level of employment in industrial countries is not really constrained by an inability to generate demand. Rather, the problem is that the governments of these countries are unwilling to allow demand to grow because of concerns about inflation. As a first approximation, one may reasonably assert that the debt crisis has had no effect on aggregate employment in the industrial world.

The real trade/finance issue is less simple. It concerns the effects of the debt crisis on the composition of employment in the industrial countries, and through this on the sustainability of the world trading system. Although the employment effects of import cuts and export promotion by debtors can be offset by employment creation elsewhere, for the individuals and firms affected the loss is nonetheless real. The political consequences are serious, particularly in the United States. With export demand from developing countries sharply reduced, U.S. firms that have relied on these exports no longer see the maintenance of a relatively open world trading system as an important objective, removing one of the main supports of a liberal trade policy. At the same time, as debtor countries attempt to increase their exports they stir up protectionist responses. These combined effects increase the strain on a world trading system that is already in serious difficulty because of the U.S. trade deficit and persistent high unemployment in Europe.

What is particularly worrisome about the trade/finance linkage is that it has the potential of feeding on itself. If the industrial countries respond to the attempts of debtor nations to run trade surpluses with protectionist measures, this will deepen the financial problems of these nations, forcing them into more urgent efforts to promote exports and restrain imports. This may seem to be an unrealistically self-defeating loop for the industrial countries to get into, but an examination of the level of much public discussion is not encouraging. Proposals in the United States for a retaliatory tariff against Brazil on the grounds that it runs an excessive trade surplus, and the uproar over increasing Mexican exports of manufactures, suggest that many influential policy-makers either do not understand or choose not to understand the trade/finance linkage.

Political and Security Consequences

An obvious and important reason for concern about the debt problem is the possibility that debt problems could lead to political instability. It is all too easy to imagine that frustration over poor economic performance in debtor nations could find its expression either in political radicalization or in nationalistic reaction.

The fact is that so far the political consequences of the debt crisis have been remarkably subdued. In Latin America the drift since 1982 has been toward increased democracy and civilian rule. Africa presents a less favorable picture. On the whole, however, the political instability that one might well have expected from the sharp deterioration of living standards and the rise in unemployment has not yet materialized.

The problem is that there is no guarantee that the political consequences of the debt problem will remain mild. Several large debtors have recently moved toward democracy, under leadership which is sympathetic toward the outlook of the Trilateral democracies. This is, from the point of view of the West, the best leadership these countries have had for a long time. If persistent poor economic performance discredits this cadre, it is unlikely that an equally favorable situation will present itself for decades to come. Thus concern about the eventual consequences of "debtor fatigue"—especially if creditor nations are increasingly seen as not living up to their side of the bargain—is or should still be a major justification for new debt initiatives and official involvement.

Social and Humanitarian Concerns

Social and humanitarian concerns as a reason for new initiatives on international debt are listed last here, not because they ought to be last in importance, but because realistically they carry much less policy weight than the other concerns. Nonetheless, altruistic interest in the welfare of others is not completely absent as a concern of advanced nations.

Where social and humanitarian concerns could play a significant role in creditor country policy is in Africa. As we have noted, African debt is small in absolute terms, constituting less than 10 percent of developing country debt and less than 5 percent of the private bank claims on developing countries. Yet the debt is a severe burden because of the poverty and faltering growth of the African economies. Indeed, for large numbers of Africans the ability of their governments to cope with debt problems may literally be a life and death issue. What this means is that debt relief that is substantial from point of view of the people of Africa might not loom large to the creditor nations.

B. THE INTERESTS OF DEBTOR COUNTRIES

Debtors have the option of unilaterally refusing to pay full debt service. The incentive for a debtor not to pay is obvious. A key question is what incentives are necessary to make this option less attractive than remaining inside the system. What are the incentives to accept the burden of debt service rather than declaring a moratorium or otherwise failing to honor the terms of the original loans? These incentives may be grouped under four headings: maintenance of current capital flows, maintenance of the option of future access to the international capital market, maintenance of trading relationships, and a set of broader concerns.

The first incentive is unambiguous: if a country is receiving current capital inflows that exceed debt service, and a failure to maintain full debt service would cut off these funds, then a debt moratorium would actually worsen the country's cash flow. Equivalently, a country has nothing to gain from unilateral action on debt if it is running a non-interest current account deficit. Here there is a sharp contrast between Africa and Latin America. The low-income African countries as a group, despite the falloff in capital inflows described above, continue to receive net inflows that substantially exceed their interest payments. By contrast, the Latin American debtors have since the onset of the debt crisis been running large non-interest surpluses, and in some cases even overall surpluses on current account.

The second incentive is a real concern but much more difficult to quantify. A country may choose to service its debt, even though this worsens its current cash flow, in order to retain the flexibility of future access to world capital markets. There are at least two levels of uncertainty about this incentive. The first is the question of how costly a loss of future ability to borrow would be. Furthermore, there is a good deal of dispute about the link between payment of debt and future ability to borrow. How long would a country that unilaterally wrote down its debt have to wait before it was once again able to raise money on international markets? For that matter, how long will it be before countries that do not take such action are again able to borrow more than enough to pay interest on their external debt? The truth is that we have very little idea. But a government is unlikely to take the risk when the consequence of a misjudgment is very severe.

Concern over trade access is a further major reason why debtors have been willing to adjust as much as they have. Under some scenarios, a debt moratorium or repudiation could set in motion a cascading series of legal actions that would strangle the country's normal channels of international trade. Whether this would happen in fact—indeed, whether creditor country governments would allow it to happen—is more doubtful, but the risk that it might happen is not something we can dismiss completely.

Finally, debtor countries, like creditors, have interests that go beyond narrow financial ones. International debt is part of a much broader network of economic and other linkages. Some of these linkages are quite direct: if Mexico or Brazil were to take a hard line on debt, they might find the United States even less forthcoming on issues of protectionism and immigration than it has been. Others are fuzzier: there is surely at least some linkage between a government's ability to appear credible in its domestic policies and its demonstrated willingness to honor international commitments.

The noteworthy point is that three of the four incentives for debtor countries to maintain debt service are of highly uncertain magnitude, and the certain incentive applies only to the low-income official borrowers. What this means is that while African debt reform must wait on the creditors, there is always the possibility that a Latin American debt initiative will take the form of refusal by the debtors themselves to pay in full. Such an action by debtors would clearly run more risks than a debt servicing procedure agreed to by all parties.

IV. Possible Dimensions
of New Debt Initiatives

We have now described the interests of debtor and creditor countries in coping with the debt problem. As we have seen, in 1983 the debt strategy adopted attempted to reach an acceptable compromise between these interests by combining defensive bank lending, additional official lending, and adjustment efforts by debtor countries. In the past two years, however, there has been essentially no new net lending by the commercial banks.[1] There is now widespread discussion about the idea that some kind of new initiative is called for. Before we can discuss actual proposals, however, we need to understand what a new debt proposal might mean since proposed initiatives range from a return to coordinated new money lending to a substantial debt forgiveness. More generally, a new debt initiative could have several possible dimensions. To introduce some order into our discussion, it will be useful to review these possible dimensions.

The essential point may be briefly stated. In the absence of a new debt initiative, debtor countries would be forced either to run unacceptably large trade surpluses to service their debt, or to declare unilateral moratoria on debt service and risk the consequences. If one proposes a new initiative, one must make two crucial choices. The first is that of procedural reform vs. reduced adjustment burden. That is, will the initiative simply try to improve the way in which the current level of financing is provided, or will it attempt to reduce the level of resource transfer that the debtor countries are obliged to make? To the extent that a debt initiative does allow countries to make smaller resource transfers, the issue then becomes one of stretch-out vs. debt forgiveness. That is, is the reduced burden on the country a temporary relief that must be compensated for by increased payments in the future, or is it provided by reducing the present val-

---

[1]After this report was drafted, the banks did agree to a two-year package of up to $7.7 billion of additional credit for Mexico. A coordinated lending agreement was also concluded with Argentina that provided for an increase in net credit.

ue of the country's obligations? Obviously a debt initiative can combine all of these features, but it is useful to begin by thinking of them separately. We present these as possible building blocks for future strategies and do not advocate any of these options. A detailed analysis of the pros and cons is developed in the next two chapters.

A. THREE BASIC ISSUES

Procedural Reform vs. Reduced Adjustment Burden
Many proposals for international debt reform call for a revision of procedures that will not affect the required trade performance of debtors—except to the extent that the new procedures work, and the old do not. A good example is a switch from year-by-year rescheduling to multiyear rescheduling agreements. This does not change the expected payments of the debtors: nobody expects that on net the problem debtors will repay principal on their medium- and long-term debt over the next several years. What it does do is to reduce the number of rescheduling negotiations that must take place, and hopefully to minimize the risk that such negotiations could break down.

Procedural reforms may be valuable, and in fact there has been some move to adopt such proposed procedural reforms as multiyear rescheduling, longer maturities on new loans, creation of secondary markets, and so on. What procedural reforms do not do is reduce the burden of adjustment on the debtor countries. If Brazil's principal is rescheduled for the next four years instead of being rescheduled in four separate negotiations, this does not change the fact that Brazil is required to run a trade surplus large enough to pay interest on its debt less any net new lending. That is, procedural reforms can deal only with technical financial issues, not with the fundamental economic problem of servicing the debt. It is of course possible that an otherwise sound debt strategy will fail because of technical issues, so that procedural reforms are not to be neglected. But if "debtor fatigue" will undermine a debt strategy that is working perfectly at a technical level, then it is necessary to go beyond procedural reform to reduce the adjustment burden.

Stretch-Out vs. Debt Forgiveness
Reducing the current adjustment burden on a debtor country—that is, reducing the size of the resource transfer that a country is required to run—means reducing the amount that the debtor pays currently to its

creditors. The issue of stretch-out vs. debt forgiveness is whether the creditors as a group are fully compensated for this reduced current receipt. In a stretch-out plan, the reduction of current debt service is in effect relent to the country at an interest rate that at least covers the creditors' cost of funds, so that the increased claims on the country's future earnings fully offset the reduced current payments. The ad hoc debt strategy since 1982 has of course been one of stretch-out, although at rates very much below the market rates that would have been required to achieve that lending on a truly voluntary individual basis. Some debt reform schemes that would radically change the nature of the debt, such as the Bailey plan described below, may also be regarded as stretch-out rather than forgiveness schemes because the new financial instruments they introduce are expected to be seen by creditors as equal in value to the conventional loans they replace.

Suppose, however, that one concludes that a debtor nation cannot even in the long run pay the present value of its current debt or should not be obliged to do so. Then stretch-out is not enough, and must be supplemented with forgiveness that reduces the present value of the debt. The best-known example of a debt forgiveness proposal currently is the Bradley proposal to convert developing country bank debt to long-term debt at an interest rate below the banks' cost of funds. Although the face value of this debt might be unchanged from the original debt, its market value would of course be less; thus in effect debt forgiveness would have taken place.

Reforming Conditionality

We have emphasized the effect of debt reform on the size of the trade balance adjustment that countries are obliged to make. In fact, however, the debt burden has not been solely defined by the trade balance adjustment. As part of the "conditionality" that the IMF imposes as a condition for lending, nations must agree to changes in specific domestic policies as well. These domestic policy changes typically include budget restriction and credit constraints as well as measures targeted at the trade balance specifically.

The important point is that the policies demanded under IMF conditionality place a high weight on fiscal discipline and control of inflation through demand restriction. Some debtors have claimed that as a result, they may have imposed more severe recessions and greater shortfalls in economic growth than were necessary to achieve the actual improvements in trade balances.

The issue of reforming conditionality is an extremely important one. To address it adequately, however, would require a careful discussion of the macroeconomics of high-debt developing countries, something that is beyond the scope of this paper. Thus our discussion of debt reform focuses on the financial aspects of reform, even though the method of adjustment may be equally important.

B. OPTIONS FOR NEW DEBT INITIATIVES:
A PRELIMINARY VIEW

In the next section we will examine explicitly the pros and cons of the most influential proposals for new debt initiatives that have been offered. It is however useful to begin with a preliminary overview of the elements that appear in many of these proposals and the basic reasons offered by their advocates. Aside from fairly minor procedural changes, there seem to be three main ideas for debt reform. The first is to change the nature of the claims that banks have on developing countries, either by handling the process of financing in ways contrary to normal banking practice or by converting bank loans into some other kind of asset. The second is to change the ownership of the claims by consolidating the debt of developing countries in the hands of a new intermediary, with existing creditors now having claims on that intermediary. Finally, the third idea is to change the value of the claims by reducing interest rates or otherwise providing debt forgiveness.

Changing the Nature of the Claims
The argument for a change in the nature of the claims on problem debtors may be considered as analogous to the argument, common in business, that the term of lending for a project should be matched to the likely returns from that project. If an investment is expected to yield returns only gradually over a twenty-year period, financing that investment with three-year loans is setting oneself up for financial trouble.

The analogy with countries is as follows: the expected net payments to creditors of high-debt developing countries are not at all well-matched with their legal debt-service obligations. Since debtor countries are expected to run current account deficits for the foreseeable future, their nominal indebtedness will grow over time. This is in fact what everyone expects, and is generally regarded as sustainable as long as GNP and exports grow faster. But, servicing the loans will require that existing debt be retired, and even if all principal is rescheduled will not allow that debt to grow. The result will be a perennial need for new financing, and thus (perhaps) a continual risk of crisis. What many reformers have proposed is that the de facto expectation that debt will grow, not shrink, be reflected in the nature of creditors' claims. Two ideas in particular have emerged. The first is that interest as well as principal be included in rescheduling agreements, so that the exposure of existing creditors grows automatically. The point is that the current debt strategy calls for new lending by the existing creditors, and this lending is to all intents and purposes forced rather than voluntary. In the view of its advocates, rescheduling interest would simply make this process explicit, and perhaps more effective.

The other principal idea is that conventional debt be converted either into equity or into equity-like claims on a country's foreign exchange earning capacity. Assuming that this capacity grows, the payments on these claims would then automatically grow over time.

Changing the Ownership of Claims
Many debt reform proposals envisage elimination of the direct claims of private creditors on developing countries. Instead, these claims would be assumed by an official agency of some kind— prominent candidates are either a new agency or a new arm of the World Bank. The private creditors would in turn acquire claims on the new agency. Some proposals add that these claims would be insured by creditor country governments.

Creation of a new official intermediary to hold developing country debt is said to be appealing for four main reasons. First, by insulating the banks from the direct consequences of any national failure to pay, such an intermediary would in effect safeguard the financial system. Second, once debt is consolidated in a single agency's hands the coordination problem discussed at length above will no longer obtain. Third, creation of an intermediary has technical advantages as a way of bypassing certain accounting and regulatory obstacles to debt initiatives. Finally, the process of transfer of claims to such a new intermediary is in some schemes also the vehicle for an official buyout of debt.

Changing the Value of Claims
Some debt reform proposals call for reductions in bank claims on developing countries, such as reductions in spreads above LIBOR and reduction of fees. The key issue is how large these concessions would have to be and whether they would be financed by the banks themselves, which is to say by their stockholders. Realistically, bank

stockholders do not themselves value claims on debtor nations at par. In principle, reductions in spreads and fees might conceivably raise the expected value of claims on debtors even though it lowers the legal obligation, and thus might not impose any costs at all.

Too large a forgiveness of debt, however, would under current circumstances threaten the solvency of major banks. Thus, official funds would have to be injected. This could be accomplished, for example, by creating a new official intermediary that buys up bank claims at a moderate discount and then restructures its claims on debtors at strongly concessional rates; the difference between the payments received by this intermediary and its obligations to the banks would then be met by creditor country governments.

C. WHO PAYS FOR DEBT INITIATIVES?

Not all debt initiatives carry a price tag. Procedural reform, if well conceived, could make all parties better off. If promises of future payments are credible, a stretch-out does not reduce the value of creditors' claims. But debt forgiveness, or a stretch-out that lacks credibility and is perceived as a write-down, involves a cost that someone must bear.

The key point here is that the structure of the debt means that private creditors can be made to bear only limited costs of debt forgiveness. Private claims on developing countries are primarily loans from banks whose capital is small relative to their assets; their deposits are to a large extent explicitly insured and to an even greater extent implicitly insured by the desire of creditor country governments to protect their financial systems. In other words, only the stockholders can be made to swallow losses, and the bank stockholders are not a large enough group to finance a total forgiveness of developing country debt. As we saw in Tables 7 and 8 above, a sufficiently large write-down would threaten the solvency of many of the largest banks.

The clear implication is that a debt initiative that involves a very large element of forgiveness would have to be officially financed. This is true even for those countries that have borrowed primarily from private lenders, and is *a fortiori* true of countries, especially in Africa, that have borrowed from official sources. Thus, to the question, who pays for debt reform, the answer must be that if the price is large the bill falls on taxpayers in the creditor countries.

V. A Survey of Major Proposed Debt Initiatives

The purpose of this section is to review some of the proposals for new initiatives on debt that have received the most attention; the advantages and disadvantages will be considered further in Chapter VI. This is not intended as a comprehensive review of all proposals, which would involve considering at least three dozen proposals, many of them similar to one another, many of them clearly misconceived. In any case, a number of surveys of this kind already exist. Instead the intention here is to discuss proposals that are both representative and at least potentially sensible.

Following our earlier discussion, the proposals will be grouped under four headings. First are proposals for procedural reform that are not intended to change the burden on the debtor nations themselves. Next are proposals to change the nature of the claims on developing countries in such a way as to reduce their current debt service without reducing the value of these claims to creditors. Third are proposals to consolidate claims in the hands of a new financial institution of some kind that becomes an intermediary between the banks and the debtor nations. Finally are proposals to forgive the debt, perhaps sufficiently so as to require injection of official money.

A. PROCEDURAL REFORMS

Multiyear Rescheduling
Continued rescheduling of debt for at least the next several years must be taken for granted even by those most optimistic about the debt situation. Since the rescheduling must happen, there is a strong case to be made for doing it now rather than in repeated negotiations. The counter-argument is that creditors want to engage debtors in frequent negotiations so as to be able to enforce sufficiently stringent adjustment policies. Increasingly, however, the control gained by this process has come to seem to some participants in the process to be illusory. Thus, multiyear rescheduling has been recognized as mutual-

ly advantageous to both sides, although the rescheduling horizons are relatively short.

Multiyear rescheduling and the next proposal, lengthening of maturities, are unique among the proposals we will consider here in that they have already been put into practice in a major way. In September 1984 Mexico negotiated a rescheduling that covered principal due over the period 1985-1990. This negotiation also involved a conversion of some debt into longer maturities. As a partial compensation for the loss of their "short leash," banks were given a mechanism for calling off the rescheduling if they are dissatisfied with Mexican policy (this process is tied to the IMF's Article IV consultations with the Mexican government).

The shift to multiyear rescheduling is, as we have noted already, a good example of a purely technical change. It does not change the cash flow position of the debtors, since there was no question that debt would be rescheduled in any case. The gain is instead one of increased certainty and reduced risk that technical factors will give rise to a crisis.

Longer Maturities

A conversion of debt to longer maturities is to some extent a substitute for rescheduling. Again, some conversion of this kind was a part of the September 1984 Mexican package.

More extensive conversion to longer maturities is a feature of a number of debt proposals. The well-known Rohatyn proposal, which we will discuss below, includes a restructuring of debt into 15-30 year bonds as one of its elements; similar lengthening of maturity characterizes related proposals by Kenen and others.

Some proposals have gone even further. In particular, Gutentag and Herring (1985) have proposed elimination of principal repayment altogether, by issuance of consols (bonds having no maturity date) to replace existing debt.

Insurance and Secondary Markets

The two proposals considered above are aimed at smoothing out the relations between banks and creditors. A different kind of technical proposal is essentially interbank in its orientation. These are schemes to help banks spread the risks of their claims on developing country debtors, either by insuring the risks or by selling some of their claims on a secondary market.

Secondary market sales are still relatively small in volume but may grow as the use of Exit Bonds permits smaller institutions to stop participating in further LDC loans. The Philippine Investment Notes are another form of secondary market security that may grow in popularity.

One might ask why these schemes require official help; why don't the banks themselves create these markets? Attempts have also been made to develop private insurance arrangements, although apparently without success. The argument of proponents of a deliberate policy of encouraging risk-spreading is that the markets are too thin, and that it is desirable to have either governments or official agencies serve as market-makers. (An alternative possibility is that the so-called moral hazard problems are inhibiting the development of these markets. We will return to this possibility in the next section of the paper.)

Insurance and secondary markets would be essentially the same in their implications for both banks and the financial system as a whole. In each case the risk of default by a particular developing country would be spread more widely, presumably both improving the position of a bank itself and also reducing the threat that such defaults could leave banks that participated heavily in North-South lending insolvent. Nonetheless, policy proposals for the two cases are quite different.

Proposals for official encouragement of insurance, advanced by among others Witteveen (1983), Lever (1983), and Zombanakis (1983), envisage the creation of an official insurance institution. This institution, in addition to charging a fee, would restrict its operation to particular classes of loans, say those associated with high-conditionality IMF programs. The important point would be, however, that in the event of a failure to pay the losses would have to be absorbed by the institution and thus indirectly by creditor country governments.

By contrast, proposals for encouragement of a secondary market, of which Gutentag and Herring (1985) is the best known, cast official institutions in the role of market-makers rather than risk-bearers. In the Gutentag-Herring proposal the IMF purchases some loans and "packages" them for resale, thereby creating a secondary market without itself taking a permanent stake in that market.

B. CHANGING THE NATURE OF CLAIMS

The purpose of changing the nature of claims on debtor nations is to bring the time profile of their debt service obligations into line with a plausible path of repayment, and thus to limit or eliminate the need for the countries to raise further new money. Proponents of these schemes typically believe that the new instruments they create will ease the problems of the debtors without reducing the value of the claims to creditors.

In a logical sense we might think of proposals for new instruments as being simply an extension of the idea of converting debt to longer maturities. However, two of the proposals we will consider—interest capitalization and indexed loans—would create a situation in which the nominal value of a claim on a debtor grows rather than shrinks over time. This is sufficiently unconventional to warrant discussion under a separate heading.

We also include under this heading three additional changes in the nature of claims held by creditors. First is conversion of debt into equity; this may, as we explain, have a substantial debt forgiveness component, but in principle at least could be simply a switch in the form of claim. Second is a conversion of debt into claims on a country's exports. Third is establishment of provisions for contingent lending by existing creditors; this establishes a new obligation by creditors, and therefore amounts to a change in the nature of their claims.

Interest Capitalization

The 1983 debt strategy relied on new lending by existing creditors as an essential ingredient. That is, in effect the strategy called on banks to convert part of their interest receipts into increased claims rather than actually collect them. At the same time, we know that such re-lending of interest depends on collective action by creditors that is difficult to enforce, and in fact the growth of bank exposure in high-debt developing countries had ceased until recently. This leads to the natural suggestion that the process of capitalization of a portion of interest receipts be made explicit. Such partial interest capitalization has been widely discussed among bankers and government officials, but has found its way into few published debt reform proposals. Three exceptions are Dornbusch and Fischer (1984), who eventually opt for a limited write-down instead, Krugman (1985), where the idea is treated favorably but no specific proposal is offered, and most recently an explicit proposal by Robichek (1985). A variant of interest capping was put forward by Massad and Zahler (1984), who advocate partial use of local currency for payment.

The advantages sought by advocates of partial interest capitalization are in part similar to those sought by advocates of multiyear rescheduling. An agreement to capitalize interest over a period of several years would reduce the need for repeated negotiations over additional finance. More important, however, is the hope that an explicit process of interest capitalization would do better at coping with the coordination problem than the informal pressures that were supposed to lead creditors to relend interest under the 1983 strategy.

Opposition to any interest capitalization stems from three sources. First, an agreement for partial interest capitalization that limited resource transfers would create pressure for complete (or more complete) interest capitalization that eliminated all resource transfers from the debtors to the creditors and that thereby put the increase in debt on an explosive path. Second, banks are concerned that if the process of relending interest is made automatic, the incentives for countries to pursue effective adjustment will be reduced. Third, capitalization of interest would raise difficult problems of U.S. accounting and bank regulation since it would go against what is normally regarded as sound practice to count loans whose interest is automatically relent as in good standing. In this context, U.S. practices are different from practices in key European countries that would permit banks to capitalize a portion of interest payments without adverse consequences for the banks' reported income or balance sheet.

Indexed Loans
One reason why the ability of countries to repay debt can be expected to grow over time is inflation, which, other things being equal, reduces the real burden of debt service. Several proposals for debt reform suggest that the time profile of debt service can be brought more into line with likely repayment paths by converting debt into loans whose principal is indexed to some measure of inflation, such as U.S. wholesale prices or world export prices. Such debt would bear a correspondingly lower rate of interest, so that initially debt service payments would be reduced. Eventually the indexation of the principal would mean larger debt service than otherwise, but this would come at a time when inflation had made such payments easier to make.

Indexed loans have been proposed as part or all of a debt strategy by a number of authors. Exactly why they have not been taken more seriously is a somewhat puzzling issue, part of the larger puzzle of why indexed financial instruments are so rare in general except under extreme inflation. In any case, the sharp disinflation in the industrial countries since 1982 and 1983 may make indexation less important than it seemed a few years ago.

Debt-Equity Conversions

A recent idea that has attracted a great deal of interest is that some debt might be converted into claims on enterprises, with dividends then taking the place of interest receipts. Several deals along these lines have already been made, although the value is still tiny compared with the debt problem.

There seem to be two advantages of debt-equity conversions. First, earnings can normally be expected to grow over time, both because companies exist in a growing economy and because of inflation. Thus, when a creditor converts debt to equity, it exchanges a constant stream of earnings for a growing one. If the two streams are to be of equivalent value, the growing stream must be smaller at first. In other words, after a debt-equity conversion we would expect the initial dividend payments to be smaller than the interest payments on the loan would have been.

This means that a debt-equity conversion serves the purpose of stretch-out: it allows a country to trade off lower resource transfer now for higher resource transfer later, when the economy is presumably more able to afford it.

In addition to stretch-out, it appears that debt-equity conversions may be being used as a vehicle for limited debt relief. The typical deal is as follows: a creditor bank sells its debt claims at a substantial discount to a firm; the firm then presents the debt to the debtor government for redemption, in domestic currency, which is then used to acquire a stake in a local firm.

Why is this debt relief? In a debtor country, where the balance of payments crisis has led to exchange control, the true value of domestic currency is less than its official exchange value. Thus, the debtor government views redemption of foreign currency debt for its par value in local currency as debt relief. The firm is willing to make this trade because it has itself acquired the debt at a discount. Finally, the bank is willing to sell at a discount because it views the prospect of future repayment as uncertain.

If debt-equity conversions are to play more than a marginal role in the debt problem, a way must be found to extend the scope for this kind of trade. In fact, proposals for conceptually similar exchanges, but on a more massive scale, do exist, and we turn to these next.

Exchange Participation Notes

One of the more intriguing suggestions for a change in the nature of claims on developing-country debtors has been the proposal of Bailey (1983) that fixed-interest claims be replaced with shares in a country's exports, which he calls Exchange Participation Notes. In effect, debt would be converted into a sort of equity on a country's whole foreign exchange earning capacity. Related proposals have suggested alternatively that debt service be limited to a fixed share of export earnings and that any difference between these payments and normal debt service obligations simply be capitalized at the loan interest rate.

The idea of Exchange Participation Notes takes the logic of matching obligations to likely net payments one step beyond indexation. It does so by taking into account not only growth in ability to pay due to inflation but also growth in real export capacity (presumably related to economic growth in general).

If there were no uncertainty, Exchange Participation Notes would amount simply to another way of achieving the same goals as interest capitalization. Since in fact the growth of exports is uncertain, however, EPNs would distribute risk differently. On one side, countries would find their risk reduced, because their obligations would vary with their actual earnings. On the other side, banks would find themselves exposed in a direct way to country export uncertainty. (It is of course arguable that given the possibility of default banks are de facto exposed to this risk in any case.)

Contingent Lending Obligations

Finally, we note that agreements that creditors will provide additional lending if specified events occur amount to a kind of contingent interest capitalization. The case in point is the recent Mexican lending package, which commits the creditors to provide additional money if either oil prices or growth fail to live up to minimum standards. Such contingent lending can be justified in exactly the same way as unconditional interest capitalization, and is subject to the same objections.

C. CHANGING THE OWNERSHIP OF CLAIMS

Many debt reform proposals have as their centerpiece the transfer of claims on high-debt developing countries from private creditors to an official institution. Such proposals may be divided into two groups. First are proposals that call for official takeover only of the incremental role of commercial banks, i.e., that call for an official institution to provide new lending to debtor nations. Second are proposals that call for an overall takeover of debt, with banks receiving claims on the new institution in exchange.

Incremental Official Lender

Two proposals for official incremental lending have received substantial attention. One is the plan proposed by Soros (1984), who proposes that a new International Lending Agency take over the role of private bank involuntary lending. The ILA would borrow its funds on the private market, enabled to do so by guarantees provided by industrial country governments. Charges on both creditors and debtors would be used to build up a capital base which would, if all went well, eventually allow the government guarantee to be withdrawn.

Mahbub ul Haq (1984) has proposed that the IMF consolidate new lending packages under a Debt Refinancing Subsidiary, which would in effect act as an intermediary between lenders and the debtor nations.

Hervé de Carmoy (1987), one of the authors of this report, has proposed a major debt program that relies extensively on incremental official lending. The de Carmoy plan proposes that the United States, Japan and the EEC assume joint responsibility for a fund which would provide resources to eligible country borrowers. The fund of $30 billion a year for ten years would be financed by the governments themselves ($15 billion per year at concessional interest rates), by the World Bank and other multilateral development banks ($7-8 billion a year of project lending), and by the commercial banks ($7-8 billion a year of project lending or trade finance). The availability of these resources to eligible borrowers would be conditional on the borrowers implementing agreed structural reforms designed to produce sustainable economic growth. The fund would be administered by an Action Committee made up of key officials of the public and private sectors and closely aligned with the existing multilateral institutions, in particular the World Bank.

There has also been considerable recent discussion of the case for creating an expanded version of the IMF's Compensatory Financing Facility, which lends to countries that have experienced temporary adverse terms of trade shocks. An expansion of this facility would represent an official counterpart to the contingent lending that we discussed as a form of changed nature of claims.

We note that Japan committed itself at the Venice Summit to recycle an additional $20 billion over the next three years to the Third World countries through contributions to the international development agencies, through direct lending by the Export-Import Bank of

Japan, and through co-financing with international lending institutions like the World Bank. Japanese commercial banks have also set up a jointly-owned factoring company to buy problem loans at a discount and thereby obtain tax relief for the participating banks.

Official Takeover of Debt

Finally we come to the most famous of debt reform proposals, the Kenen (1983) and Rohatyn (1983) plans.

Kenen's plan is the milder of the two. He calls for the creation of a new entity, the International Debt Discount Corporation, which would offer to buy up loans to a specified list of countries at a modest discount from face value (10 percent in the original proposal). The discount would allow the IDDC to offer some interest forgiveness to the countries; the IDDC would also extend the maturity of debt.

Rohatyn's plan similarly calls for a buyout of debt by an official agency—he suggested the IMF, the World Bank, or a new agency created for the purpose. In contrast to the Kenen plan, however, this agency would buy debt with its own, low-interest bonds, presumably implying that banks would take a substantial capital loss (although this loss might be minimized for accounting purposes). The agency would then offer debtor countries both a stretch-out of debt and a reduction in interest rates, with the intention of reducing debt service to no more than 25 to 30 percent of exports.

To reduce debt service to the levels suggested by Rohatyn would require that either the discount at which debt is acquired be large, or that there be a substantial injection of official funds in some form. While no formula is proposed, Rohatyn has made it clear that he would envisage that some of the losses would be absorbed by industrial country governments rather than by the private creditors.

D. CHANGING THE VALUE OF CLAIMS

The final category of possible debt reform is that of debt relief pure and simple: reducing the obligations of debtor countries so as to provide a reduction in their debt service obligations at creditors' expense.

In the first few years of the debt problem few proposals allowed explicitly for any debt forgiveness. On one hand, the size of developing country debt relative to bank capital and earnings was so large that it seemed that debt forgiveness large enough to provide much relief to the debtors could not come entirely at the expense of bank stockholders without threatening the stability of the international financial system. On the other hand, the political climate was and is very unfavorable for any official injection of funds that can be seen as a bailout for countries or banks. Thus, most debt reform proposals have sought a "technical fix" that avoids the necessity for a large reduction in the present value of debt.

Recent developments have led to renewed advocacy of debt forgiveness for several reasons. First, as we showed in Table 8, money center banks have raised their capital faster than their developing country exposure, so that they are not as vulnerable to insolvency from a write-down of this debt. Second, lower world interest rates in nominal terms mean that a substantial reduction in the burden of resource transfer can now be achieved with a smaller proportional interest reduction, and therefore less reduction in the capital value of bank claims, than was possible a few years ago. Finally, the difficulty of getting banks to increase their exposure over time, and the continuing lag in debtor country growth, raise doubts about the continuing feasibility of schemes that do not provide some debt forgiveness.

An interest write-down proposal was offered by Dornbusch and Fischer (1984), who proposed that interest rates on developing country debt be reduced moderately for only the next few years. The intent was to provide some immediate debt service relief but to limit the impact on the value of loans sufficiently that the solvency of banks was not put at risk.

Congressman Schumer (1983) proposed a comprehensive interest rate reduction for troubled debtors, sufficient that together with a stretch-out of maturities the burden of debt service would be reduced to levels comparable to those in Rohatyn's plan. The problem of bank solvency was not treated in his proposal, though the magnitude of the debt relief would surely make this an issue. The widely discussed Bradley plan is a direct descendant of this approach.

Finally, we have already noted that the Rohatyn plan contained a major element of debt relief.

VI. EVALUATING DEBT INITIATIVES

We have now described some of the major proposals for new initiatives on international debt. Our next task is to ask how these proposals stand up given the conceptual framework developed in the previous section and the facts of the situation as described earlier.

The purpose of this discussion is, as we emphasized at the beginning of the report, to provide an analytical basis rather than to make a final pronouncement.

A. PROCEDURAL REFORMS

Our discussion of procedural reforms mentioned multiyear rescheduling, extension of maturities, and the closely related issues of secondary markets and insurance. The first two seem clearly sensible and as we noted have already to some extent been put into effect. Insurance and secondary markets are, on the other hand, of much more questionable desirability.

Multiyear Rescheduling and Extension of Maturities
The argument for multiyear rescheduling and for lengthening of maturities is the straightforward one that problem debtor countries will not repay principal on net in the medium term whatever the banks do. Since this is the reality, one might as well recognize it explicitly and avoid unnecessary negotiation—saving political and managerial resources for issues where the outcome is in fact negotiable.

The argument against this is the desire to maintain ongoing negotiations, as a way of enforcing discipline on the debtor's policies and also giving debtor governments a rationale for pursuing politically unpopular policies.

Secondary Markets and Insurance
Several proposals urge that creditor governments and/or multilateral lending agencies encourage spreading of risk, either by acting as market-makers for secondary markets in developing-country loans or

by providing new insurance facilities. Whether or not this is a good idea depends crucially on the form of the overall debt strategy. If involuntary defensive lending remains a key element, as in the 1983 strategy, these proposals could easily be counterproductive.

There are two cases for encouraging a secondary market or insurance scheme. The first is the belief of some analysts that by allowing a wider sharing of risk, this would encourage increased new lending to problem debtors. The second is the belief that risk-spreading would lessen the vulnerability of the financial system to a debt-created crisis.

The first of these arguments is incorrect. Under normal circumstances an increased ability to diversify risk may encourage new lending. For lending to problem debtors, however, the obstacle to voluntary lending is not the uncertainty but the expected return: claims on high-debt countries are not regarded as worth their par value, and no potential lender will voluntarily choose to convert a dollar into 60 cents, even if the 60 cents are risk-free. This also means that an insurance scheme, unless it is intended to serve as a disguised subsidy, will have to involve very high premiums—high enough so that the cost of insuring a dollar's worth of claims is enough to reduce the value to something like 60 cents. Clearly, availability of such costly insurance will not bring new lenders into the market.

The second argument may have some validity. As we have seen, the risks to the financial system posed by developing country debt stem not so much from the sheer size of that debt as from the way its ownership is concentrated in the hands of a few highly leveraged banks. It is possible that with well-developed secondary markets and/or insurance these vulnerable banks would choose to accept some losses or pay some insurance premiums in order to reduce their exposure, and that this would have the systemic benefit of reducing the risks of insolvency among major banks.

The major problem is, however, that the concentration of debt in the hands of a relatively small group, while it increases systemic vulnerability, is also a key to the maintenance of involuntary lending, which was essential to the 1983 debt strategy and remains important in conventional initiatives such as the Baker Plan. As we have seen, there is a conflict between the collective interest of creditors, which may call for defensive lending, and the individual interest of particular banks. To overcome this conflict requires coordinated action on the part of the banks. If the ownership of claims on debtors becomes more widely diffused, the coordination problem becomes more severe—and we have seen that it is already severe enough that involuntary lending other than to Mexico has ground to a halt.

In fact, we might argue that secondary markets or insurance would pose a "moral hazard" problem. Existing creditors who sold off some of their claims or took out insurance would then have a reduced incentive to participate in rescheduling and new loans. This would in turn reduce the value of the loans sold through the secondary market and reduce the expected return of the insurers.

B. CHANGING THE NATURE OF CLAIMS

We have discussed five types of changed claim—capitalization of interest, indexed loans, debt-equity conversion, exchange participation notes, and contingent lending obligations. Since indexing has lost some of its interest with lower inflation, however, let us focus on the other four.

Interest Capitalization

The case for partial interest capitalization, like the case for multiyear rescheduling, is that it simply makes explicit something that must happen in any case. In the absence of interest forgiveness the nominal debt of developing countries with debt problems must be allowed to grow over time, and thus some relending of interest is essential. Why not, then, make the process explicit? There are two advantages to doing this. The first is the usual one of avoiding repeated renegotiations that take valuable managerial resources and also run the risk of a rupture. The second is that an explicit process of interest capitalization might help to "lock in" banks that would otherwise be failing to participate in the provision of new money, eliminating the coordination problem.

A primary argument against any interest capitalization is that once the practice of capitalization is permitted it is difficult to contain it. If the banks permit 30 percent of the interest to be capitalized, the debtors might demand 50 percent or 100 percent.

A further argument against interest capitalization rests on technical accounting grounds. The de facto interest capitalization under the 1983 debt strategy, in which "new money" provided by existing creditors was used to pay interest, allowed U.S. banks to continue to report all of their interest receipts as income. Under current U.S. banking regulations explicitly capitalized interest could not be counted in this way, so that banks' reported income would drop. Since banks are in fact uncertain about the extent to which their claims will in the end be honored, the current practice certainly overstates bank earnings; but counting none of the interest that is capitalized would go to the other extreme and would understate earnings.

Another argument against interest capitalization is once again that borrowers would not be required to negotiate at regular intervals to obtain needed credit. If the provision of new money is made institutionally too easy, debtor countries will not make sufficient adjustment efforts.

The problem is that the system of relending to cover part of interest, which was designed among other things to avoid the accounting problems associated with involuntary growth in exposure, has not been working. Banks have not been expanding their exposure at anything like the rates that would keep resource transfer at tolerable levels. Thus, the case for taking interest capitalization seriously is stronger now than it was in 1983, unless the banks follow the 1986 Mexico precedent and increase their net lending to other major countries.

Debt-Equity Conversions
As we have argued, debt-equity conversions in principle allow a mixture of stretch-out and debt relief. Since there is a reasonable case for both of these, debt-equity conversions appear to be a useful innovation. It is possible, however, that they may lead to increased capital flight or the "round-tripping" of the equity inflow, as noted in the part of Chapter II on capital flight (pages 28-29).

Exchange Participation
The appeal of exchange participation notes or some other system that allows debt service to grow with the economy may be most strongly conveyed by returning to our numerical example of debt service and resource transfer. Recall that we assumed a country whose dollar GNP was growing at 7 percent per year, with a debt equal to one-half of GNP, paying an interest rate of 9 percent. Even with complete rescheduling of principal, full payment of interest would require resource transfer of 4.5 percent of GNP. Given the growth of the economy, however, the relative size of this burden would fall in half every ten years. The country might well prefer a more level burden of resource transfer.

Suppose now that all of the debt were converted to Bailey-style Exchange Participation Notes, entitling its owners to a fixed share of export revenues. If exports are expected to grow at the same rate as GNP, 7 percent, so will earnings on the notes. A straightforward calculation shows that the owners of the notes should consider a 1 percent share of GNP as valuable as the original debt. Since 1 percent resource transfer is a fairly modest number, the debt problem would thus seem to be solved.

This is not merely an accounting trick. In fact, the reasons that the case for Exchange Participation Notes looks so favorable are precisely the reasons that calculations such as those of Cohen (1985) and Feldstein (1986) suggest that developing country debtors ought to be solvent: the ultimate burden of servicing debt is greatly reduced by growth.

Despite the apparent favorable aspects of an exchange participation scheme, Bailey's proposal and other related ones have met with a generally negative response. There are three main complaints about this kind of scheme.

The first criticism is that the novelty of proportional claims on national export earnings would disturb financial markets, leading to an excessive depression in the value of bank stocks.

The second criticism is that proportional claims on a country's exports would not be credible; if exports were to grow rapidly, countries would then be unwilling to honor their commitments. This may be true. However, conventional loans also have this problem, in reverse, in that countries become unwilling to honor them if exports are low. One might suppose that the incentive to meet foreign obligations and thus retain normal access to world markets would be stronger for countries doing well on those markets than for countries doing poorly, and that the exchange participation might therefore be if anything less subject to sovereign risk than fixed-interest loans.

Finally, an objection to any shift to a new form of asset is that it would force an accounting change. As long as the claims of banks on developing countries are not transformed, and as long as the secondary markets remain marginal, the banks can carry the loans on their books at face value. With a change in their nature the loans would probably have to be "marked to market," revealing a significant capital loss. If other objections to exchange participation are surmounted, however, this loss need be no larger than the losses that are already built into bank stock prices. While there is a good case for avoiding underreporting of banks' true earnings that would result from interest capitalization, it is not clear what purpose is served by seeking to avoid reporting a loss which is genuine (in an expected sense at least) and is probably already discounted by the market.

Contingent Lending

An arrangement that specifies that creditors will lend to a country in the event of adverse circumstances, like interest capitalization, may be defended as a useful way to build in something that must happen in any case if a strategy of defensive lending is to work. If the price of oil drops again Mexico will have to be provided with new money; why not formalize this contingency now rather than run the risk of a failure to reach an agreement under pressure.

The argument against this is once again that it eliminates periodic negotiations and therefore the pressure for debtor country reforms. In the current case, however, this view is less compelling, since the contingent lending is intended to deal with contingencies outside the country's control.

C. NEW INSTITUTIONS

Many plans for wholesale debt reform stress the creation of new institutions in whose hands debt would be consolidated. Despite the wide attention given to these plans, however, the advantages and disadvantages of a new official intermediary have not been as clearly discussed as they should be. We will discuss these advantages and disadvantages in general, then turn briefly to the content of some actual proposals.

Advantages of a New Intermediary

Why is there any advantage in converting the direct claims of banks on countries into claims on an intermediary which in turn becomes the new creditor? Most proposals for such an intermediary are not too clear on this, but we can in fact identify at least four advantages (which must of course be set against disadvantages).

The first advantage is that once debt is concentrated in an intermediary's hands, the coordination problem will of course cease to be an issue. This advantage depends, however, on getting those creditors that would otherwise refuse to participate in new lending to be part of the consolidation, which may not be easy. Precisely those banks that are most likely to be able to extract themselves in the absence of an intermediary will also have the least incentive to transfer their claims to that intermediary. Thus, this advantage may not be as easy to grasp as one might imagine.

The second advantage is that to the extent that a debt initiative does involve an element of officially financed debt relief, an intermediary provides an easy channel for this relief. For example, in Rohatyn's plan the new institution buys out bank claims with bonds that offer less than market interest rates, and in turn reduces the interest rates on developing country debt. An official contribution to debt relief would then naturally take the form of a subsidy that allows the institution's lending rate to be below its borrowing rate.

The third advantage is in fact closely related: an official intermediary would offer a more attractive channel than other options for insulating the financial system from the effects of a major repudiation or write-down of developing country debt. Since the losses would now occur in the first instance to the intermediary rather than to the banks that have become its creditors, industrial country governments would be able to insure the banking system's solvency by aiding the intermediary, rather than having to undertake the de facto nationalization of the banking system that we described above.

The final advantage is a technical one, but possibly quite important. Creation of an intermediary might serve as a way to cut through the accounting and regulatory objections to unconventional schemes such as interest capitalization and exchange participation. Since this may not be obvious, it deserves a little more discussion.

Consider the example of interest capitalization. As we saw, this could have a devastating impact on the reported earnings of banks, because none of the capitalized interest could be counted as income. Suppose, however, that banks exchange their claims for claims on an official intermediary. There is then nothing to prevent the intermediary from allowing debtor nations to capitalize some of their interest. To do this would require that the intermediary initially be able to borrow so as to pay interest to the banks; if claims on the intermediary are guaranteed by a consortium of governments, as they would have to be in any case, this should not be a problem.

Disadvantages of an Intermediary

The most obvious disadvantages of an intermediary are that its creation might turn into a bailout either for the banks or for the countries. In addition there is the problem, stressed by Cline (1984), that consolidation of bank claims would take banks "off the hook," eliminating the possibility of new involuntary lending.

The concern about a bailout for banks is certainly justified. Developing-country creditors do not expect with certainty that they will be repaid; as we have seen, secondary market evidence suggests that much of the debt is subjectively discounted by 30 percent or more. A buyout by a new intermediary at anything close to par would thus indeed constitute a bailout. Thus, in order to avoid a bailout it would be necessary that an intermediary make an effort to buy debt at a discount comparable to what it would have been worth otherwise. Many observers are skeptical about whether this is actually the way it would turn out. We may note, however, that we have a reasonable idea about what value banks place on their developing country claims, and a buyout at much more than this would be conspicuous and would not go unremarked in the U.S. Congress and elsewhere.

The concern about a bailout for countries is equally realistic, and perhaps not as easy to assuage. Basically the worry is that an official creditor would not be as tough as private claimants. Without the incentive of profit or the risk of bankruptcy, and with foreign policy concerns tending to impinge on financial ones, an official intermediary might tend to let debt restructuring slip into debt forgiveness on a scale unintended by its founders. Against this all one can suggest is that the example of the IMF shows that it is not impossible to create multilateral agencies that are fairly tough-minded. In particular, any new organization would be under the baleful eye of a populist U.S. Congress, so that with appropriate institutional design one might not have to worry about excessive willingness to give money away.

Beyond these concerns is the point emphasized by Cline, that debt consolidation will give creditors a chance to wash their hands of the debt problem and thus to cease involuntary lending. This point needs to be understood clearly. It has two aspects: the known need for an expansion of exposure, and the need for flexibility.

The first point is the familiar one that to keep the resource transfer problem manageable without substantial debt forgiveness we must find a way to allow the nominal indebtedness of problem debtors to grow rather than shrink over the near future. Under the 1983 strategy this was supposed to be dealt with by new involuntary lending by existing creditors. Once these existing creditors have exchanged claims on the countries for claims on an official body they have no further stake in the countries and thus no incentive to continue lending.

This means that any new lending after a debt consolidation must come from official sources. The most plausible source is the new intermediary itself, which now has the same stake in defensive lending that the original creditors had. The problem is that in order to make this new lending the intermediary must itself borrow new money. It is not clear why this should be regarded as an insuperable problem.

Admittedly, the new lending will take place at an expected return below market rates, because of the continued risk of nonpayment; but if the intermediary was brought into existence properly it will have been compensated for this in advance by the discount at which it acquired bank claims.

A stronger argument is the loss of flexibility. If unanticipated developments required more lending than initially anticipated, the original creditors would no longer be on call to provide more involuntary loans. Again, however, what this requires is that the intermediary itself be able to borrow; if this can be arranged, there is no reason why the intermediary cannot then capitalize interest or make new loans. When it does this, of course, it will take losses in an expected sense. On the other hand, favorable developments will constitute gains for the intermediary. Ideally, the discount at which the debt was acquired will offset the expected losses, though actual losses may be either more or less.

It is clear that many things could go wrong in the establishment and operation of a new intermediary. It would be misleading to assume that everything could be made to work out perfectly. On the other hand, a realistically skeptical view about such an intermediary should not be contrasted with an idealized view of the 1983 debt strategy, which has also not worked out as it ideally might.

D. DEBT RELIEF

As we have noted, only recently has the idea of offering substantial debt forgiveness been seriously discussed in political circles. Since some kind of debt relief at some point in the future is at least a possibility and clearly has its current advocates, the prospect needs to be discussed. It should of course be stressed that forgiveness of debt is fundamentally different from a write-down of debt on the banks' own balance sheets or an increase in reserving by the banks against the risks of future default.

The original Kenen plan and to some extent the Rohatyn proposal were designed to forgive enough debt to bring the debt service down to a level where it would be payable out of current export earnings. The advocates of these plans seem not to have appreciated the size of the capital losses that would be implied by such a reduction. Although the decline in interest rates since 1984 has made the size of these capital losses a good deal smaller, they are still very substantial.

To understand the relevant magnitude, let us return to our example of a country with debt equal to 50 percent of GNP. Let us suppose, as in many recent proposals, that the plan is to convert debt into long-term bonds with a below-market interest rate, where the rate is set low enough to reduce the burden of resource transfers to levels that are sustainable without new borrowing. How much will the present value of the claims have to be reduced?

The answer depends on three things. First is the initially prevailing interest rate; we will again assume a 9 percent rate. Second is the maturity of the new bonds; we will give calculations for 15 years and 30 years. Finally is the level of the "acceptable" resource transfer; we consider resource transfers of 2 percent of GNP and of 3 percent of GNP.

Limiting the resource transfer to 3 percent of GNP and using 30-year bonds reduces the value of the banks' nominal claims by 38 percent. A 15-year maturity would cut the value of the banks' nominal claims by 51 percent. And limiting the resource transfer to 2 percent of GNP (15-year maturity) would increase the loss to 67 percent of the current nominal value.

A further basic criticism of large-scale debt forgiveness is that it is unnecessary because of the likely improvements in the ability of the debtor countries to service their own debts. Converting the debt into long-term loans without providing a supply of new money for the near term requires countries to run a constant nominal resource transfer despite the fact that their exports can be expected to increase in volume and price. The alternative of allowing debt to expand would keep the initial debt service burden manageable without such a large reduction in the present value of the banks' claims. This thinking underlies both the 1983 debt strategy with its reliance on involuntary coordinated lending and such unconventional proposals as interest capitalization and exchange participation.

An additional criticism is that any such partial reduction in the value of the debts would lead to demands for further debt relief. If the banks are willing to forgive 30 percent of the debt, why not 50 percent or 70 percent? Finally, such imposed debt reduction schemes would almost certainly eliminate the availability of new private money for an extended period of time.

An alternative to explicit debt forgiveness would be the decision of the creditor banks to sell loans from their portfolios at a price that was less than par but not less than the current secondary market rate. The debtor countries could then purchase these loans at their reduced values. Since the countries had not actually defaulted on their debt, there would be no legal obstacle to resumption of lending. At the same time, if the reduction in the debt burden were sufficient to restore confidence, new lenders might once again be willing to come forth. Of course, relying on all of this would be taking a serious risk.

A second alternative would be to rely on official lending to reduce the cash flow burden after a moderate debt relief. The lending could take the form of conventional new loans or, alternatively, if the debt were assumed by a new official intermediary, the intermediary could engage in interest capitalization or even exchange participation. There is however no reason to believe that such official lending is available since it would appear to be an unnecessary bailout of either the lenders or the debtors or both.

VII. CONCLUDING COMMENTS

As we stressed in the opening section of this report, we believe that the debt problem of the developing countries must be solved in a way that is consistent with achieving solid economic growth in the debtor countries and improvements in the financial positions of the creditor institutions. The past five years have in fact seen a mixture of successes and failures, of progress and of disappointments. We are now at a point where the future is uncertain.

New steps must be taken to assure that progress will be made in the years ahead. Although the Baker Plan correctly called for a combination of new lending and debtor country reforms aimed at achieving economic growth, the plan did not actually elicit any net new lending in the 18 months after it was proposed. Very recently, however, the banks did agree to a two-year package of up to $7.7 billion of new net credit for Mexico. The Government of Mexico has also taken several major steps to improve its domestic economic performance. The question now is whether the other debtor countries will also undertake appropriate policy reforms and whether the banks and the official lending agencies will together provide enough credit to permit a desirable rate of economic growth.

Although the four authors of this report are not unanimous in our diagnosis of the present situation and in our prescription for the future, we do agree on several key points. We agree that there is no simple global solution and that each country must be treated as a separate case on its own merits. We also all believe that the debtor countries will need additional credit in the years ahead to help offset their interest payments and that the rate of growth of new lending proposed in the Baker Plan is likely to be inadequate for achieving a desirable rate of economic growth. We recognize the desirability and potential importance of steps to reverse the flight of capital from the debtor countries that has occurred in recent years and to augment external credit with increased direct investment from abroad. This in turn underscores the importance of improved domestic policies in the debtor countries, a subject which lies outside the scope of this report. Finally, we agree that explicit debt forgiveness would be unwise.

Where we disagree is about just how much credit the debtor countries will need to achieve satisfactory growth, how willing the creditor banks will be to provide the necessary amount of credit, and what the prospects are for substantial public funds to supplement private lending.

Three of us believe that, if the banks and the multilateral creditors are willing to increase their nominal lending to the debtor countries at a rate that keeps the real value of the debt approximately constant, the debtor countries will have enough external credit to sustain a healthy rate of economic growth. If this occurs, the debt will decline as a proportion of the debtor countries' GNP and of the exports of those countries. Thus, the debtor countries will find it easier and easier over time to service this enlarged debt and the creditor banks will find that the ratios of that debt to the banks' assets and earnings will also decline. Although there are clearly financial and political difficulties in getting the creditor banks and the debtor governments to cooperate in such a plan, we believe that such cooperation is feasible and in the best interests of all the parties. Insurance, official guarantees or co-financing arrangements with the World Bank and other agencies may help to elicit such increased nominal lending.

One of the report's authors, Hervé de Carmoy, is less sanguine than the rest of us about the current situation. He believes that much larger credit increases are needed to achieve satisfactory growth in the debtor countries (he proposes new lending of $30 billion a year, a nominal rate of increase of about 10 percent in real terms) and that about three-fourths of that additional credit should come from multilateral agencies like the World Bank and from the major industrial countries, including a substantial proportion at concessional rates of interest. Without such lending, the burden paid by the debtors will become politically unacceptable as the restoration of voluntary market lending remains too far distant in the future. Moreover, de Carmoy doubts that the degree of cooperation between debtor governments and creditor banks envisaged by the rest of us can be achieved. And by not providing sufficient resources now an important opportunity to give fresh momentum to sustainable economic development and contribute to global political and economic stability is missed.

The other authors doubt the need for such large increases in credit. Moreover, they also doubt the feasibility of obtaining such credit from governments and multilateral agencies. The formidable obstacle posed by political opposition to government provision of additional finance is also recognized by de Carmoy, but if the problem is indeed as large as he believes, then he believes it is necessary to call for political vision and statesmanship to be given precedence over political expediency.

Although the primary responsibility for successful agreement on the future of the debt lies with the bilateral negotiations between the debtor countries and the commercial banks, an important role has also been played by the International Monetary Fund, the World Bank, the Paris Club and the individual central banks. This is proper since the interests of the creditor nations are more than the interests of the individual banks or even the banking system as a whole.

A general problem in the current situation is that, while each debtor country must be treated on an individual basis, the political nature of the debt problem makes it difficult for the political leaders of a debtor country to accept less favorable terms in a debt rescheduling than have been given to other creditor countries. This makes it hard for the creditors to provide lower interest rates or partial debt forgiveness to some countries without providing that same treatment to other debtors as well.

The difficulty of organizing new private credit for the debtor countries is due in part to differences among the banks. The tax and accounting rules differ among the major creditor countries in important ways which influence the reserves that the banks have taken, the cost of providing new money and the most appealing form of rescheduling arrangements. A greater harmonization of these accounting and tax rules could lead to an increased availability of funds for the debtor countries.

The future of the international debt situation is uncertain. Despite the current slow pace of activity in the world economy, appropriate actions by the debtor countries and by the creditor institutions can lead to healthy economic growth in the current debt-laden countries, a gradual reduction in the relative burden of servicing that debt, and a strengthening of the creditor financial institutions. A failure to achieve these improvements would not only destroy the opportunities for economic growth in the debtor countries but could also undermine the political democracies of Latin America and the strength of the world's financial system. The resolution of the debt problem in the next few years will therefore remain one of the world's central economic and political issues.

APPENDIX

The Origins of the Debt Problem

The main text of this report has focused on the handling of the debt problem since the onset of crisis in 1982, rather than on how the debtor countries came to acquire an unsustainable debt burden in the first place. For the medium-term management of the debt problem, the existence of the debt is simply a fact we must face. For the longer term, however, it is important to understand what went wrong. This is not a matter of apportioning blame; it is, instead, a matter of figuring out what features of the international system led to an outcome that in the end left everyone in difficulties.

The rise in lending to developing countries during the 1970s was part of a general opening of international capital markets. As late as 1981 many observers still saw the new-found ability of developing countries to borrow extensively on private markets as beneficial both to lenders and borrowers. The transformation of this apparently favorable development into a crisis rested on four factors: a deterioration in the external environment; policy errors in the debtor countries; errors in judgment by banks; and policy errors in the industrialized countries.

External Factors
Changes in external factors had a dramatic impact on the debtor countries but were essentially beyond their control. The crucial developments were:

- *Higher real interest rates.* These rose from an annual average of 0.7% in 1973-1980 to an annual average of 6.7% in 1980-1985. Nominal interest rates rose from 8.4% in 1973-1980 to 12% in 1980-1985. The sharp rise in international interest rates was also accompanied by a strengthening of the U.S. dollar (in which most debt was denominated), which further added to the burden.
- *Lower commodity prices.* With the onset of recession, the decline in real commodity prices gathered pace. From 1980 to 1982, prices fell by almost 15%, to a level 23% below the previous peak of 1977 and almost 39% below the 1974 peak.
- *Recession.* The tightening of monetary policy to halt inflation produced the worst recession in the United States since the 1930s. Growth in the industrialized economies slowed to 1.2% in 1980 and 1.4% in 1981, and fell by 0.4% in 1982. Moreover, world trade was also badly hit, expanding by only 1.7% in 1980 and 0.8% in 1981, and contracting by 2.3% in 1982.

Various studies have attempted to quantify the impact of these variables. Cline (1983) calculated that the increase in real interest rates, the loss in export volumes as a result of the recession in industrialized economies, and the decline in commodity prices had cost the non-oil developing countries $141 billion. Sachs (1985) has estimated that the increase in real interest rates in 1979-83 cost the equivalent of 1.3 percent of GNP of six Latin American countries. This same group experienced a 1.2 percent terms of trade improvement, but this was essentially due to gains for Mexico and Venezuela from the rise in oil prices. Other debtors suffered losses ranging from 4.9 percent of GDP (Chile) to 2.3 percent (Brazil). Maddison (1985) found that there was a loss in real income in five Latin American countries of 2.1 percent in 1979-83 as a result of changed terms of trade. The differences in these studies reflect differences in methodology but all confirm the substantial impact of these developments on the debtor countries.

These studies are also revealing in two other ways. First, LDC debtors which did not experience debt-servicing problems—including South Korea, the third largest borrower from commercial banks—suffered a deterioration in these external factors on a scale similar to that experienced by the rescheduling borrowers. Second, some of the debtors that experienced debt-servicing problems (e.g., Mexico and Venezuela) had a marked improvement in their terms of trade. This implies that external factors were not the only cause of the debt problem.

Policy Errors in Developing Countries

Until the sudden shift in the global economic environment, the inadequate policies of developing country debtors had not been apparent. Moreover, with very low or even at times negative real international interest rates, developing country borrowers, like everyone else, had every incentive to borrow and little incentive for economic managers to run a "tight ship," especially if that meant unpleasant political choices. But, in the changed environment policy errors were starkly revealed, as the inflationary cushion for economic policy-makers disappeared.

In the countries where debt servicing problems have occurred, foreign savings began to replace domestic savings and the incremental capital-output ratio was generally higher than in those countries without debt-servicing problems. It took more of a given stock of capital to produce the same unit of output. Thus, there was inefficiency of investment and some wastage of the foreign financial flow.

It is equally clear that these countries did not devote sufficient resources to creating the kind of technological base or industrial capacity that could generate a high level of foreign exchange earnings, reduce imports and significantly increase the genuine creation of wealth. It is no coincidence that the volume of exports of debtors with rescheduling problems grew at an average annual rate of 0.75 percent in 1973-82, compared with an average annual rate of increase for debtors without rescheduling problems of 4.75 percent.

Moreover, most of the debtors that incurred problems experienced severe capital flight, a feature which has still not been eliminated in some key countries. Estimates of the amounts involved vary and usually comprise some assets that are held abroad for healthy economic reasons (e.g., to advance export credit, to provide working balances, and to maintain a balanced portfolio). The Institute of International Finance, for example, has calculated that private sector asset flows abroad in the largest five Latin American debtor countries amounted to $101 billion in 1979-84, compared with a debt inflow of $188 billion in the same period.

Insufficient attention given to technology, inefficiency of investment, low growth of industrial and service exports and capital flight were usually associated with over-large budget deficits and overvalued exchange rates. And, most of these countries had relatively high and unstable inflation rates.

It is also clear that the debtors who later had servicing difficulties undertook very little adjustment during 1979-82 but, instead, borrowed heavily to finance wider current account deficits. Thus, the current account deficits of the debtors with problems rose from 17.5 percent of GDP in 1979 to 30 percent in 1982, while those without allowed their current account deficits to increase from only 8 percent to 9 percent in the same period.

One area where the evidence is less clear-cut is in the role and size of the public sector itself, rather than the public sector deficit. Many countries that did not experience debt-servicing problems had a relatively large public sector presence in critical areas, as measured for example by public investment as a share of total investment.

Bank Lending

Lending by commercial banks generally exceeded what could be considered prudent. This is reflected in the concentration of loans to individual countries relative to individual banks' capital. Implicitly this has been recognized by the regulatory authorities who in some countries, for example the United States, have explicitly instructed banks to improve capital ratios within a given time frame, or have insisted on provisions against new loans to certain countries (e.g., in Canada).

With hindsight, risk evaluation techniques were not wholly adequate. The perception that lenders need not carry out in-depth analysis and be guided by its conclusions may have had its roots in certain "fallacies" related to this lending. First was the sovereign borrower fallacy. This argued that sovereign lending was relatively low risk because "countries do not go bust." Second was the commodities fallacy. It was often assumed that because a country had plenty of "resources in the ground," especially oil, it must have a bright future. Third was the umbrella fallacy. This related to the belief that either the United States (e.g., in the case of Mexico) or the Soviet Union (e.g., in the case of Poland) stood behind certain debtors and would "bail them out." Fourth was the "short-leash" fallacy. This contended that by lending short-term rather than long-term, banks remained more liquid and, therefore, an individual bank's exposure could be reduced before problems arose. To these fallacies could also be added what has been termed "disaster myopia," grossly underestimating or ignoring the probability of a rare but potentially disastrous event occurring, in other words, reducing the probability of it occurring to zero. There may also have been an element of belief that banks themselves would be bailed out by some kind of lender-of-last-resort, providing a form of moral safety net. Finally, with regard to project lending, there was a failure to identify adequately the risk that a country would not make foreign exchange available to service the loan for a specific project which was otherwise viable.

Nevertheless, although with hindsight banks left themselves vulnerable to fundamental changes in their external environment, this was far less clear at the time. First, since the shift to a disinflationary environment and the profound impact it would have on real interest rates and commodity prices was not predicted, there was a false sense of security. Secondly, with very low or negative real interest rates, the borrowers, whatever their weaknesses, appeared to be essentially solvent.

The Role of Industrialized Countries

Aside from the impact of economic policy actions, government officials in the major economies actively encouraged the belief by the commercial banks and the borrowers that having completed one round of "recycling" after the first "oil shock," another could be attempted successfully after the 1979 "oil shock." Lord Lever and Christopher Huhne (1985) have made a useful collection of quotations from leading officials at the time. Two are reproduced here:

> The private markets have also served us well in the continued success of the recycling process....[T]he success of both newly industrializing and middle-income countries in attracting private capital, particularly bank lending, reflects their ability to offer opportunities for profitable and productive investment. This has enabled them to finance their external payments and raise their living standards and is surely the best form of recycling. (Sir Geoffrey Howe, U.K. Chancellor of the Exchequer, Autumn 1981)

The impression I get from the data I have reviewed is that the recycling process has not yet pushed exposure of either borrowers or lenders to an unsustainable point in the aggregate, especially for the American banks, whose share in total bank lending to non-oil developing countries in recent years has declined and whose share of claims in those countries in total assets has also declined. But problem cases exist now and will no doubt continue to show up. (Paul Volcker, Chairman of the U.S. Federal Reserve Board, March 1980)

The multilateral institutions also failed to detect sufficiently early the incipient crisis. The IMF (1986) admits that "...while Fund surveillance resulted in the transmission of warning signals to certain debtor countries in the context of Article IV consultations, it did not produce the perception of a global debt problem until a relatively late stage." The major forecasting bodies, including the OECD and the IMF, projected continued large OPEC surpluses on the back of high oil prices and failed to detect the size of the 1980-82 global recession, the depth of the decline in commodity prices and the strength of the surge in interest rates.

REFERENCES

Bailey, Norman A. 1983. "A Safety Net for Foreign Lending." *Business Week*, January 10.

Bergsten, C. Fred; William R. Cline; and John Williamson. 1985. *Bank Lending to Developing Countries: The Policy Alternatives.* Washington: Institute for International Economics.

Cline, William R. 1983. *International Debt and the Stability of the World Economy.* Washington: Institute for International Economics.

Cline, William R. 1984. *International Debt: Systemic Risk and Policy Response.* Washington: Institute for International Economics.

Cohen, D. 1985. "How to Assess the Solvency of an Indebted Nation." *Economic Policy*, November.

de Carmoy, Hervé. 1987. "A Proposal for Dealing with the Debt Problem." Paper prepared for 1987 Trilateral Commission Task Force on Restoring Growth in the Debt-Laden Third World. New York: Trilateral Commission

Dornbusch, Rudiger and Stanley Fischer. 1984. "The World Debt Problem." Report prepared for UNDP/UNCTAD and the Group of 24. Cambridge: Massachusetts Institute of Technology. Processed.

Feldstein, Martin. 1986. "International Debt Service and Economic Growth: Some Simple Analytics." National Bureau of Economic Research Working Paper No. 2076. Cambridge: NBER

Guttentag, Jack and Richard Herring. 1985. "The Current Crisis in International Banking." Washington: Brookings Institution.

ul Haq, Mahbub. 1984. "Proposal for an IMF Debt Refinancing Facility." Address to UNESCO, July 6.

International Monetary Fund (IMF). 1986. *World Economic Outlook.* Washington: IMF

Kenen, Peter B. 1983. "Third World Debt: Sharing the Burden, A Bailout Plan for the Banks." *New York Times*, March 6.

Krugman, Paul R. 1985. "International Debt Strategies in an Uncertain World." Cuddington and Smith, eds. *The International Debt Problem.* Washington: World Bank.

Kyle, S.C. and Jeffrey D. Sachs. 1984. "Developing Country Debt and the Market Value of Large Commercial Banks." National Bureau of Economic Research Working Paper No. 1470. Cambridge: NBER

Lessard, Donald R. and John Williamson. 1985. *Financial Intermediation Beyond the Debt Crisis.* Washington: Institute for International Economics.

Lever, Harold. 1983. "The International Debt Threat." *The Economist,* July 9—a somewhat revised version of his presentation to the Trilateral Commission Rome meeting in April 1983.

Lever, Harold and Christopher Huhne. 1985. *Debt and Danger.* London: Penquin Books

Maddison, Angus. 1985. *Two Crises: Latin America and Asia, 1929-38 and 1973-83.* OECD Development Centre Studies. Paris: OECD

Massad, C. and R. Zahler. 1984. "The Process of Adjustment in the Eighties: The Need for a Global Approach." *ECLA Review,* August 23.

Robichek, W. 1985. "External Debt Relief." *Journal of Development Planning,* no. 16.

Rohatyn, Felix. 1983. "A Plan for Stretching out Global Debt." *Business Week,* February 28.

Sachs, Jeffrey D. 1985. "External Debt and Macroeconomic Performance in Latin America and East Asia." *Brookings Papers on Economic Activity,* no. 2.

Schumer, Charles E. 1983. The Schumer proposal is described in H. Erich Heinemann, "Third World Debt Problem: Governmental Role Urged," *New York Times,* March 10; and also in "Flexibility is the Answer," *Journal of Commerce,* April 13.

Soros, G. 1984. "The International Debt Problem: A Prescription." New York: Morgan Stanley Investment Research Memorandum.

Witteveen, Johannes H. 1983. "Developing a New International Monetary System: A Long Term View." Per Jacobsson Lecture, September.

Zombanakis, M. 1983. "A Way to Avoid a Crash." *The Economist,* April 30.